To Chris

It was a pleas...

...you at Witch...

...BB. Fred ...

RELIGION
without
BELIEFS

Frederick Lamond is one of the foremost international authorities on Paganism, and his deep knowledge of the craft is illuminated by frequent contact with Pagan groups to whom he lectures all over Europe and America.

An economics graduate of Cambridge and Chicago, Mr Lamond has practised Wicca continuously since 1957, when he was initiated into the movement by Gerald Gardner. He is a longstanding member of the Fellowship of Isis and the California-based Church of All Worlds.

RELIGION
without
BELIEFS

*Essays in pantheist theology,
comparative religion and ethics*

Frederic Lamond

JANUS PUBLISHING COMPANY
London, England

First published in Great Britain 1997
by Janus Publishing Company
Edinburgh House, 19 Nassau Street
London W1N 7RE

British Library Cataloguing-in-Publication Data.
A catalogue record for this book is available from the British Library.

ISBN 1 85756 341 7

Cover design Harold King

Photoset by Keyboard Services, Luton
Printed and bound in England by
Antony Rowe Ltd, Chippenham, Wilts

Acknowledgements

I should like to thank all those who have given their time to read the manuscript of this book and to suggest much needed improvements: especially my wife Hildegard, Prof. Ronald Hutton of Bristol University, Christina Oakley, Karin Rainbird, Prudence Jones, Fleur Shorthouse, Michael de Ward, Heide Patterson, Karin Forrester, Francesca De Gradnis and Anna Korn.

Table of Contents

	Page
Introduction	ix
I The End of Absolutes	1
1. The Dance of Shiva	3
2. Lessons of the Fall	13
3. The Christian Heritage	23
II The Worship of Life	39
4. Experience	41
5. The Goddess	59
6. The Horned God	71
7. Ethnic Gods and Goddesses	79
8. Community Festivals and Worship	96
9. Pagan Ethics	106
10. Pagans and Other Religions	116
Summary Table of Characteristics	143
III Handling Power	145
11. An Initiatory Path	147
12. Do Spells Work?	159
13. The Sacred Marriage	177
Bibliography	182

Introduction

In the flurry of new religious movements of the last 40 years one stands out for its unusual features. It recognises no living or dead masters or divine avatars, has no holy scriptures, dogmas or required beliefs; indeed no authorities of any kind outside the direct personal experiences of each practitioner.

Yet despite this philosophical anarchy these personal experiences are sufficiently similar to allow members to join together in small home-based groups and large festivals to celebrate our common reverence for life and nature. We thus gain all the social and spiritual benefits of belonging to a religion.

Nor is this religion theologically impoverished by a reduction to the lowest common denominator. We have embraced the rich pantheons of the European pre-Christian religions and – at times – of contemporary Hinduism and African religions, not as beliefs but as poetic descriptions of our relationship to our living environment. That is why we call ourselves Pagans and our religion Paganism.

It is said to be one of the fastest growing of the new religious movements and has certainly become much more visible in recent years. This has aroused the interest of liberal Christian vicars and theologians, religious sociologists and anthropologists. Christian and Pagan weekend meetings have taken place in southern England since September 1994 to promote greater mutual understanding. It is to these interested outsiders that this book is primarily addressed, comparing our theology and ethics with those of the mainstream Jewish and Christian religions.

The book is divided into three parts. In the first, I look at contemporary Western society and its spiritual needs, and speculate on why the established churches no longer seem able to satisfy those of more than a small minority. These are personal views, not backed by any in-depth surveys of opinion, but they are shared by many in the Pagan community.

In the second part I describe contemporary Western Paganism, and the convictions, attitudes and ethics that all Pagans share: the solitaries as well as the members of covens, groves and nests; the laymen and women as well as the initiates of the various Pagan mystery traditions. But I also describe such differences of approach and practice as exist, and the reasons for them.

Finally, in the last part I describe my own Wiccan tradition: the spiritual path and ideals it offers its initiates; the purpose of its spellcasting and other magical practices; and why these have to remain secret. I also discuss its potential as a priesthood to the wider Pagan community, and what priesthood could mean in such an individualistic and self-reliant movement.

Books about religion have to steer a narrow course between two extremes. If they seek to describe a religion in abstract, intellectual and theological terms, they risk leaving out any feeling for its spiritual and emotional life, and the meaning that it gives to its participants' lives. But if they are wholly subjective, they cut off any point of contact with other religions, any basis for a discussion of comparative beliefs and ethics.

I have tried to do both therefore. I begin the first two parts with descriptions of some of my own and other Pagans' personal mystical experiences that made us aware of our pantheist religious feelings, and later confirmed us in them. I have also included personal experiences in other chapters where they were useful to illustrate certain practices and attitudes. But otherwise I try and describe Paganism as objectively as possible, to allow theologians and religious psychologists to place us in the spectrum of human religious attitudes.

Christian priests and ministers, Jewish rabbis and Muslim mullahs will find plenty in this book with which to disagree and even to deplore. Let them debate these differences frankly with us and criticise us – if they must – for what we really affirm and do. But let them refrain from projecting their own inner demons on us: unfounded calumnies lower their image as well as our own in the public eye, and do a grave disservice to the cause of religion in our all too secular society.

Let them also ponder the words of the Pharisee Gamaliel to the Jerusalem Sanhedrin trying Jesus' followers.

> If what is being planned and done is human in origin, it will collapse. But if it is from God, you will never be able to stamp it out, and you will risk finding yourself at war with God.

I have tried to show in our personal experiences that our movement does indeed have a divine origin, in the universal Life-Force we call the Goddess.

Wernberg, Austria, 1996

I

The End of Absolutes

1

The Dance of Shiva

At the beginning of 1958 I was returning one night from a lecture on comparative religion in Central London to the caravan in which I lived in Bricket Wood, not far from St Albans in Hertfordshire. I did not own a car in those days, and buses ran only as far as Garston Garage after 11 p.m., so I set out to cover the last two miles on foot. It was a clear, full moon night with only the odd wisp of cumulus cloud passing across the moon's face like a caress. As I walked along the A405 I contemplated the moon absent-mindedly as I wrestled once more with the problem that had been nagging me in recent weeks.

Following my initiation into witchcraft the previous year, I had partly worked out, partly received in sudden flashes of insight, an intellectually satisfying cosmotheology that seemed to answer all human history's ethical conundrums rather well. But how could I know that my conceptual structure was the right one, and that all the great minds that had contributed to Christian theology over the last two millennia – Paul, Augustine, Thomas Aquinas, Luther, Calvin and many more – had implicitly been wrong? Wasn't this rather childish hubris?

As I looked up at the moon, my mind wandered to a contemplation of the eternal ballet of interlocking circular dances performed by the heavenly bodies: the Moon revolving around the Earth every 29.5 days, the Earth around the Sun every 365 days, and – who knows – perhaps the Solar System itself around some larger unseen centre of attraction. These revolutions bear a strong resemblance to those performed by the electrons around the nuclei of the atoms in each cell of our bodies, and in all energy and matter.

Could it be that the Solar System, and each of the other stars visible to us, are only atoms in a cell of the body of some giant being, in whose life the whole of known cosmic and terrestrial history is but a short breath? Conversely, are whole races and civilisations rising and falling every second on each electron of each atom of my body? Does the Universe fold into itself not just in space, but in such a meeting of the infinitely large with the infinitesimally small?

This speculation seemed to unlock a door of consciousness. Like Cocteau's Orphée, I suddenly walked through the mirror out of space and time. Leaving my body walking along the A405 far behind, my consciousness expanded to encompass the whole sky, and then the whole Universe.

I was the calm placid Moon which I had been contemplating so intently, the fiery furnace of the Sun, the whole Earth and its mountains and valleys, rivers, lakes and seas, and the mighty forces that had moulded it and all the other planets of the solar system, and all the other stars and their planets and satellites. I thrilled to the ecstasy of their dance, and each of their revolutions was like one of my breaths.

Then suddenly the cosmos within my consciousness was filled with all the souls of all the sentient beings that had ever lived and ever would live, and I was every one of them. I was every king and queen, general, priest, artisan and peasant since the dawn of history, as well as every beast, bird and insect of the forest. I was every passionate pair of lovers of every race and animal breed since the beginning of time, and every couple of parents tenderly nurturing their young.

But I was also every lion and tiger chasing a gazelle, and every gazelle being chased. I was full of the terror of villagers overrun by a plundering army, but I also thrilled to the soldiers' excitement in their pillage and raping. I was every Jew

4

starved or gassed to death in a Nazi concentration camp, but also every one of their SS guards.

I was the One Soul of the Universe, the deepest part of all beings, that has always been and always will be, and survives the death of mortal bodies and their egos and even of the planets on which they live.

The vision began to fade, and far below me I became dimly aware of a pair of feet walking along a country road. Then I remembered the intellectual problem that had been bothering me and began to match every religious myth, belief and dogma that I could think of against the fading vision of universe and eternity. To my shocked surprise, they *all* fitted!

Christian beliefs that had defied all logical reasoning suddenly appeared easy and self-evident. Had I been an anguished would-be Christian wrestling with intellectual doubts, these would have been washed away and I would have returned from the experience joyfully proclaiming I had 'met Christ'. But I had long ceased to be a would-be Christian and I continued to match against the fading vision Jewish, Muslim, Hindu, Buddhist, Taoist and old Mediterranean polytheistic beliefs. They all fitted equally well.

The heavenly choirs of the Christian paradise described the ecstasy of unity with the cosmos as well as but no better than the Mohammedan paradise in which one is attended by beautiful houris, or the land of rest and recuperation for tired souls on the far shores of the Styx, or the Buddhist nirvana, or the Hindu dance of Shiva.

Desperate for some guidance, I started reciting theological propositions that in terms of human logic are mutually exclusive:

'There is but One God.'

True.

'There is an infinite number of gods and goddesses struggling with and loving each other, and Life as we know it is the fruit of their interplay.'

Equally true.

'There is no God.'

Just as true.

5

'Good and Evil are opposite forces, forever struggling for the soul of humanity.'

True.

'Good and Evil both derive from the One, and are equally important aspects of the divine scheme of things.'

True.

By then the vision had faded completely, and I was wholly back in space and time. Looking about me to locate myself, I reckoned I could not have walked more than four paces during the entire experience. Dazed I continued on my walk home.

For the next three days I seemed to move about my daily routines in a state of moral weightlessness, with all the moral and ethical programming of my childhood wiped out. I had been given complete freedom of choice.

On the positive side I had lost my fear of death and of the destruction of life by a nuclear holocaust. I now *knew* spiritually and emotionally what until then had only been an intellectual postulate: the essential part of me was immortal and eternal and would survive the death of my physical body and its conscious memories. Death would be but the final curtain on my current role on the stage of life, and the prelude to learning a new one. Even if our asinine governments blew the world up in a nuclear holocaust and thereby brought the higher forms of mammal life to an end, I would still be there among the forces present on the irradiated Earth, helping to initiate a new cycle of evolution.

I had also lost the somewhat élitist fear shared by many university graduates: that of losing my identity in the vast sea of suburban middle-class mediocrity in which I commuted every day to and from central London. As I travelled to and from work I looked on my fellow passengers in a new light. Behind each one of those conventional clothes styles and closed expressions was another incarnation of the One Soul of the Universe, with his or her own unique set of gifts and handicaps, joys and sorrows, set of friends, lovers, spouse and children, whose experiences might well be a more entertaining act for the One than my own.

This newly found security did not wholly compensate, however, for the terrifying amorality of the One that I had experienced, and the equally frightening freedom of moral choice that it gave me. I felt free to become a social predator, victim, healer or detached observer. I could join the Foreign Legion or a criminal fraternity, or a secret police force holding down an oppressed majority in the interests of a favoured few, or a revolutionary, or a member of a religious order devoting itself to the relief of hunger and suffering, or of an enclosed contemplative order. Or I could lead a conventional middle-class life as breadwinner of a nuclear family. Each role would be equally valid in the light of the experience I had just had, an equal contribution to the infinite diversity of Life that it would thereby affirm, as long as I had freely chosen it for myself and enjoyed it. Boring oneself and thereby the One watcher within was the only sin.

My own choices had in the past been in the direction of idealistic activism: for European federalism in my student days; more recently, seeking the pattern of religious beliefs that would best help human beings pursue knowledge and a rising standard of living in harmony rather than in conflict with each other and with Nature. Seeing these ideals put on a par with those of all the forces of oppression and conflict by the all-encompassing all-seeing but detached One, as just some of very many games and roles on the stage of Life, seemed suddenly to rob them of all dignity and meaning.

My grandmother had once told me an old Jewish tale of a young man who, driven by insatiable curiosity, broke the greatest of Torah taboos and peered behind the veil hiding the Ark of the Covenant. What he saw made him faint. When he recovered, he never smiled nor spoke again but lived the rest of his life with an expression of infinite sadness on his face. If he saw what I had seen, I could see why.

Three days later, I was still as dazed by my experience as I had been immediately afterwards. Then suddenly it was as if a voice spoke in my head to say:

'You have had a glimpse of the Infinity beyond Space and

the Eternity beyond Time, to which you will return at the end of your physical life. But you cannot go on living on that plane without going mad. You have been incarnated as a time- and space-bound human being of flesh and blood in a time- and space-bound material world with a purpose to fulfil, and you must accept the limitations of your condition, including the apparent logical mutual exclusiveness of different aspects of the Eternal reality.

'You cannot, therefore, live by all the aspects of Infinity and Eternity at once, but must choose which partial aspect you will live by. Choose carefully, because while some aspects of the Eternal reality can help you live a fuller, more effective and happier life, others could destroy you and the world in which you live. Trust your own inner sense of Truth to guide you: the aspects of the Infinite reality that can help you will appear to you spontaneously as "true", while you will be instinctively repelled by those dogmas, beliefs and ways of life that are destructive of your integrity, health and those of the world in which you live.

'In thus choosing the mental constructs and myths most suitable to your age, do not be so arrogant, however, as to proclaim them "truer" on the plane of Eternity than other beliefs chosen by other men living in other times or cultures than your own. If they chose differently from you, it was not necessarily their inner sense of Truth that was deficient, just the circumstances of the age in which they lived which called for a different response.'

The Multiplicity of Truth

The inner voice gave me a huge sense of relief. I did not have to prove Paul, Augustine, Thomas Aquinas *et al.* to be deluded in order to validate my own Pagan cosmology and Wiccan practice. Their ages were indeed vastly different from my own, and may well have required a different religious response. Whether the Christian Church's intolerance and cruelty to different believers at the height of its power was ever justified is a question that can be left to a later chapter.

The vision itself had taught me that an Infinity without spatial boundaries and an Eternity without temporal limits can be experienced in mystical visions of a few seconds; but is incommunicable, to those who have not experienced it, in language designed to describe spatially- and temporally-limited beings, objects and experiences. This point has already been made by other writers on 'peak experiences', notably Maslow.

The most that prophets and theologians can achieve is to describe one small aspect of the Infinite reality by analogies drawn from our mundane experience. The curse of such formulations in a spatially- and temporally-limited language is that they appear to deny other equally true aspects of the same Infinite reality. A statement such as 'There is one God' affirms the unity and interdependence of all parts of the visible Universe and of the power that created it in the first place, but appears to deny the infinite variety of spiritual as well as physical beings and objects to be found within it.

If we now describe this marvellous diversity as a pantheon of gods and goddesses loving and fighting each other in a very human manner, this in turn appears to deny the cosmos' unity. And when the atheist denies the Church's authority to impose its theology on him by affirming 'There is no God' (external to me and the created universe) he appears also to deny the existence of any integrating and purposeful power at the Universe's centre, and plunges his listeners into existentialist despair.

Poets and mythmakers who appeal to the heart and the imagination have a better chance of squaring this circle than theologians who seek for formulations that will satisfy the rational mind. But it is as absurd to affirm that only one religious myth can be valid, as it would be to say that only one love poem can convey the ecstasy of human passion. Those churches and philosophical systems that claim a monopoly of the ultimate truths know nothing of the Universe's awe-inspiring complexity; nor are they interested in it, but only in exercising power over the ordinary people of their societies.

The Relativity of Truth

If the vision of Shiva's dance firmly rejected all religious or philosophical totalitarianism, the inner voice in the end also rejected the lazy contemporary liberalism that regards all religions as equally good and subject only to individual preferences and tastes. This is a useful position for keeping the state out of regulating its citizens' worship, and has been the bedrock for the freedom of religions enshrined in the United Nations' and European Declarations of Human Rights. But our personal standards for choosing our religious practices and communities should be more exacting.

Religious beliefs and practices are not gratuitous aesthetic choices. They provide a mental map for our understanding of the society and universe in which we live, and thus condition our responses to them. As my inner voice said, some such responses can 'help you live a fuller, more effective and happier life, others could destroy you and the world in which you live'. Religions are potent socio-psychological mechanisms for good or evil: we must choose them with care.

The Inner Sense of Truth

How? As individuals we can only trust our inner sense of Truth, which seems to be constantly testing our inherited religious maps against our daily experiences, in a similar manner to the scientist performing endless laboratory experiments to test scientific theories that he has been taught or that were suddenly revealed to him in a flash of insight. As long as the experiences remain compatible with one's religious map, this will continue to appear spontaneously 'true'. But when changing personal and social circumstances or scientific discoveries can no longer be squared with an inherited or acquired religious world-view, this will suddenly appear less true, and inner doubts will multiply among the religion's adherents.

For a while, they will try and hide their doubts from each other and even from themselves so as to be able to continue to enjoy that religion's social benefits. This is when intolerance of non-conformists will spread, because the person with different beliefs or none reminds the doubter of his own inner doubts; people at peace with themselves are rarely intolerant of those with different myths from their own. But when doubts become so widespread that that religion's members can no longer hide them from each other, the religion's hold on the imagination and loyalty of its adherents will rapidly unravel, and participation in its organised worship and festivals will fall to a small proportion of nominal members.

The Behavioural Effect

Theologians, religious psychologists and anthropologists wonder at the factors that cause such sudden declines of religious structures that had held good for centuries. Let them try considering the behavioural effect that different religions have on their members, and that dominant religions have had on the societies that they dominated.

Not the behaviour that they preach from pulpit or in ashrams: they all recommend love of one's neighbour, charity, tolerance, motherhood and apple pie; but the actual behaviour of the broad mass of their adherents. Ignore the extremes: the small numbers of saints and demons found in every religious tradition. Concentrate on average behaviour: the peak in the distribution curve of patterns of behaviour.

Christianity's cultural effect on European and European-settled cultures has been very different from Islam's on the countries of the Middle and Far East, or Hinduism's on India, Buddhism's and Taoism's on China. Within Christendom, the predominantly Protestant countries of the last four centuries have produced different cultures and economies from those that remained predominantly Catholic.

What may be the socio-psychological causes of these differences? The number and gender of the deities worshipped? The character and related life of the mythical founder? The recommended sexual ethic and marital customs? There is a rich field of study here awaiting the specialist: the sociologists

11

Weber and Tawney pointed the way in their study of Protestantism. Their conclusions may no longer be universally accepted by contemporary religious sociologists, who have found the causal connection between Protestant doctrine, Western individualism and capitalism far more complex than Weber and Tawney had described them. That is no reason for giving up the study of the relationship between religious practices and social behaviour, or for refusing to formulate alternative theories.

Now compare these diverse cultural and economic effects with contemporary society's needs. Some may be just what we most need today, others would be distinctly deleterious. Do not be surprised if it is the religions whose usual social effects are the least desirable today which are declining.

2

Lessons of the Fall

In November 1989 we all thrilled to the collapse of the Berlin Wall and the Communist dictatorships in Eastern Europe. Since then we have witnessed the failure of the August 1991 coup and the disintegration of the old Soviet Union. The end of the Cold War and of thermonuclear confrontation between the erstwhile superpowers has made the world an immeasurably safer place than previously. The Iraqis, Kurds, Croats and Bosnians might not think so, but the wars from which they have suffered since the Communist collapse – however nasty and brutish – do not threaten the survival of the human race. Throughout Europe and most of the world, therefore, there should now be more reason for hope than there has been for forty years.

A Solely Economic Failure?

Economic bankruptcy was the immediate cause of the Communist system's collapse. Not only could it not satisfy any but the population's most basic necessities; it had never been able to do so. It could no longer even produce military hardware to match the West's, despite the unreasonable priority that paranoid system had always given to military expenditure.

Most commentators – not least in the erstwhile Socialist

countries – have therefore concluded that it was Socialism *as an economic system* that failed. With a touching faith in the superiority of Western economic methods, and pushed by their peoples' demand for Western economic abundance, the new Eastern European and Russian governments are therefore switching to pure capitalist economics in its most extreme Thatcherite form. Meanwhile, in Western European elections the failure of Eastern European Socialism is being used by Conservative and Liberal parties as a stick with which to beat their Social Democratic adversaries.

This theory is unproven. Mixed economies that include both Socialist and capitalist elements have worked perfectly well in the Scandinavian countries for sixty years and in Continental Western Europe since the end of World War II. They have offered health and social services of a quality well beyond that enjoyed by most citizens of the erstwhile Socialist countries, as well as unemployment benefits that take the edge off the fear of starvation for both the temporarily and the long-term unemployed. Yet this social security has not prevented productivity and standards of material consumption from growing in these countries, as smoothly as in the less diluted capitalist environments of the United States and, more recently, the United Kingdom.

The True Culprit: single party totalitarianism

It wasn't their welfare services, therefore, which caused the East European and Soviet socialist economies to fail. Nor was it the nobility of the socialist ideals of economic egalitarianism and working for the community rather than private profit: these have been shared – at least until recently – by most West European socialist parties, which continue to enjoy con-siderable electoral support.

The real difference between Western Europe and socialist Eastern Europe is that the former has been free and democratic in the last 40 years, with free elections at periodic intervals at which citizens could choose among *several* political philo-sophies and parties; whereas the latter was under the tyranny

14

of a *single* party, the Communist Party under its various national names. Where other Christian Democratic and Liberal parties were allowed to survive in Eastern Europe, it was only as Communist Party satellites, whose leading role they were obliged to acknowledge within Popular Front coalitions.

The Communist parties based their arrogant claim to a monopoly of intellectual influence and political power on the nobility of their ideals, and on the 'historical inevitability' of their triumph throughout the world. All alternative viewpoints on economic and political affairs were suppressed by censorship and the secret police: there could thus be no feedback from the citizenry. This freed the Party and its appointed governments to pursue the most dogmatic economic policies, irrespective of their consequences.

In the Soviet Union and in Czechoslovakia, state ownership of industry, commerce and services was ubiquitous so there was no opportunity for individuals to try out new ideas at their own risk. Those who did so regardless were prosecuted and imprisoned as 'speculators'. In the other so-called 'popular democracies' limited private enterprises were allowed: up to five employees in Poland and Hungary, even up to 100 employees in East Germany until the early 1970s, hence a rising East German standard of living in the 1960s and early 1970s. But when the East German private enterprises showed the 'People's Own' enterprises up by being more innovative and efficient, producing goods of a higher quality, the Honecker regime reacted by nationalising them in the mid-1970s. After that, it was downhill economically all the way.

With all opposition and criticism suppressed, the ruling Communist parties felt they could ignore people's needs indefinitely. At no time have they offered their citizens more than the most basic shelter and food requirements, but the Party apparatchiks and industrial managers did not feel like sharing the same austerity: so secret networks of shops appeared in which insiders could get all they wanted, thus undermining the system's own proclaimed ideals.

With no tangible rewards for hard work and initiative, the

population lost all interest in creative or efficient work. 'They pretend to pay me, so I pretend to work for them!' was a common Polish attitude as far back as the 1960s. Eventually this was bound to undermine even the Socialist economies' capacity to satisfy their military priorities and the Communist officials' privileges: hence the recent economic collapse.

When the populace started demonstrating in the streets of Leipzig, Berlin and then Prague, it was primarily for the right to form alternative political parties and for freedom of travel, expression and the press. These were also the greatest achievements of former President Gorbachev's perestroika in the Soviet Union, for which the Russians will be forever grateful to him. It was to defend these rather than incipient capitalist enterprise that the citizens of Moscow defied the tanks in August 1991 and caused the old guard's coup to fail. And it is for their sake that the Russians are putting up with the economic privations that the chaotic move to a free market is causing them.

And it is because it freed our fellow Europeans in the East to speak and write their minds and to form political parties that public opinion in the West unanimously applauded the fall of the Communist dictatorships. On their countries' moves to extreme economic liberalism opinion, here like there, is much more divided.

Spiritual Bankruptcy

The industrialised capitalist West, which the newly liberated East Europeans and Russians are trying so hard to emulate, is not without its problems. Our industries may be humming and filling our shops with an abundance and variety of goods undreamed of in erstwhile socialist Eastern Europe. In Western Europe, the social services may be providing an efficient cushion against starvation, but the signs of social stress are everywhere: falling standards of education in overcrowded classrooms, growing drug consumption, both legal (alcohol and tranquillisers) and illegal, especially among teenagers; rising divorce, suicide and crime rates; growing homelessness

16

and people sleeping rough. But above all, a sense of hopelessness about the future, despite the end of the Cold War.

'Spiritual bankruptcy' is the term most commonly used to describe the state of the West. In Europe at least, churches and synagogues are emptying of all but the old and a small number of committed young. This has undermined the morale of their leaders, who are becoming increasingly uncertain what sort of spiritual and moral lead they ought to be or indeed are capable of offering. Religion may never have interested more than a minority of the European population; but the more integrated sense of purpose of that minority allowed it to influence the social tone. It is that minority which has now lost its bearings.

Industry and commerce are doing their best to fill – and exploit – this spiritual void by offering a vision of ever-rising comfort and material consumption in American shopping malls and their European imitators. Some social psychologists have commented that these have taken over many of the churches' traditional functions as social focuses. The weekly family shopping trip, even when there are no needs to satisfy, has become a kind of religious ritual, in which the participants get the feeling of belonging to a larger whole.

The consumer society cannot, however, act for long as an effective religious surrogate. It can only quieten the aching spiritual void in most people's minds by offering ever-rising material expectations to everyone: and that means ever-rising mass consumption of limited natural resources, which could be exhausted during the next century, side by side with ever-growing pollution by carbon gases and industrial waste. Growing awareness of and concern for phenomena like global warming, the holes in the ozone layer above the Earth, and the decimation of the rain forests, are contributing to a widening feeling of discouragement about the future, which is dissipating the hope engendered by the spread of political freedom to the erstwhile Socialist bloc.

The Lure of India

Just as economically starved East Europeans have long regarded the affluent West as their Mecca, so the most sensitive and adventurous among the spiritually starved North Americans and Western Europeans have found their external spiritual ideal: India, land of gurus, to which European and American students flock in their thousands every year in search of enlightenment.

From a rational materialist point of view, this ideal is odd. India has appalling social problems. Nowhere in the world is the gap between the richest and the poorest so great, and the poorest in a lower state of degradation. The richer European and American classes may be lacking in sensitivity and concern for the poor of their countries at times; but they do not deliberately set out to deprive them of water, nor chase them out of churches, as some of the upper-caste landowners of North India do to their lower-caste neighbours.. The growing number of beggars sleeping rough on Western cities' streets is distressing, but none of them feels it necessary to blind or cripple their own children to get larger alms.

The relationship between Western brides and their mothers-in-law may often leave a lot to be desired, but when did a European or American mother-in-law last set her daughter-in-law on fire in order to free her son to get another bride with a larger dowry, as frequently happens in Delhi? Women are far from having achieved professional and economic equality with men in Europe and North America; but for over two thousand years, neither have European widows been expected to jump on their dead husbands' funeral pyres, as they still are in some Rajput villages.

And yet, side by side with these horrors, there is indeed in India a richness of spiritual life that is palpable to any visitor: not only in the splendid temples of several different religions, which are full of worshippers at all times; but at the numerous colourful and joyful religious festivals; and in forest clearings where one will often encounter a meditating *saddhu* – exuding

18

tranquillity, spiritual integration and power. India is spiritually to the West, what the West is economically to erstwhile socialist Eastern Europe.

Multiplicity = Abundance

To what does India owe its spiritual richness, which is not shared by its Muslim neighbours? Does any Western seeker go on spiritual pilgrimages to Pakistan or Bangladesh? The only difference is that Pakistan and Bangladesh are Muslim and, therefore, as monotheist as the erstwhile Christian West. But in India there is a multiplicity of religions, and the dominant Hindu religion is itself polytheist. Is India's spiritual richness due to the large choice of deities and religious paths for the would-be devotee, just as the West owes its material abundance to the freedom of many producers and suppliers to compete in the same markets for the satisfaction of consumer needs?

Monotheism/Monopartyism = Bankruptcy

If so, we have a ready-made explanation for Western Europe's and North America's spiritual impoverishment: the monotheism practised by their dominant religions, especially since the Protestant Reformation, just as Socialist monopartyism impoverished Eastern Europe and Russia economically.

For monotheism and monopartyism both derive from the same authoritarian mindset. This decrees that only *one* of the infinite variety of possible mental structures for understanding the Universe, lifestyles and forms of economic organisation, can be the true one and should, therefore, be the only one to be officially tolerated.

Eastern Europe and Russia have been impoverished by the attitude of the Communist bureaucracies. For respectively 40 and 70 years, these were less concerned with satisfying their citizens' economic needs than with preventing anyone outside the Communist state power structure from doing so.

In the same way, the Christian churches have long been more concerned with hunting down heresies, i.e. unauthorised

19

spiritual paths, than with fulfilling their worshippers' spiritual needs. Some do so to this very day: while all churches sorrow at their empty pews and the materialism of contemporary society, these do not fill them with the alarm and anger expressed by Evangelicals at young people's growing interest in the occult.

The parallels between Communist and Christian practice are anything but fortuitous. The Reverend Donald Soper, Moderator of the (English) Methodist Church, has pointed out that Marxism looks like a secularised Christianity. Both Christianity and Communism have preached the brotherhood of mankind, spread education and taken practical steps to alleviate the worst kinds of poverty and suffering. But both have also used this noble ideal as the justification for persecuting those who preached different paths. The Inquisition was the KGB's forerunner, the Albigensian Crusade and the witch hunts the models for the liquidation of the kulaks. And both have pointed the eyes of their faithful to a distant utopia (after death, or for the next generation but one) to make their present oppression more tolerable.

Christianity's Greater Resilience

Whereas the Communist system collapsed after a mere 70 years in power in Russia, Christianity has survived for over sixteen centuries since Constantine made it the Roman Empire's official religion.

Communist power collapsed within a few years of President Gorbachev's removal of the fear of the secret police in Russia. But when state power stopped backing the Christian churches' religious and philosophical monopoly two hundred years ago, the churches survived and the Victorian period even saw occasional revival movements on both sides of the Atlantic.

Corruption and cynicism at the highest levels of the Church hierarchy contributed to the Protestant schism nearly 500 years ago. This changed the forms of worship in Protestant countries, but did not undermine the Christian faith as such among the religious-minded Europeans. Indeed, it is paradoxical that the present decline in Christian worship and belief should be occurring at a time when leading churchmen are men of greater integrity and selflessness than at any time in its history. What have been the causes of its past success, and its contemporary failure?

Have Scientific Discoveries Undermined Christian Faith?

The most common explanation is that Darwin's Theory of Evolution, and archaeological and anthropological theories about the Earth's and humanity's age, have undermined acceptance of the Book of Genesis. But this will only apply if its account of the Creation is taken literally and factually, as only Christian and Jewish fundamentalists believe (to the probable astonishment – if they were here to witness it – of the Chaldean and Israelite story-tellers who first related this myth).

Seen as myth, the Genesis Creation is in no way disproved by modern scientific discoveries. What it says in poetic form is that the Creation (= evolution) of the Universe and the Earth were purposeful and planned beforehand by a higher Creative power, whose existence the churches have admittedly not been able to prove; but scientists have not disproved it either, few actually having tried to do so.

Scientific Method versus Scriptural Dogma

There is a much more serious incompatibility between the method used by the physical sciences to prove or disprove theories, and the churches' method for resolving disputes about beliefs or practical morals.

The scientific method is *pragmatic*. Laboratory experiments are endlessly repeated to ascertain whether certain actions always have the results predicted by the theory being tested. If any results ever fall outside a predicted range, other than those predicated by chance alone, the theory has to be modified to accommodate the new results. This is the method which we have all learned at school and to which we owe all the great scientific discoveries of recent centuries, and the technologies

21

based on these to which we owe our present standard of living.

The Christian, Jewish and Muslim theologians' method by contrast is *scriptural* and *dogmatic*. Whatever is written in the Torah, the Bible or the Qur'an must be believed and/or obeyed, even though it was written thousands of years ago by priests or prophets living in totally different circumstances from our own. For instance, the Roman Catholic Church's opposition to the remarriage of those divorced people whose marriage had been blessed in a Christian church while their former partner is still living – a practice shared by parts of the Anglican Church – is not based on the insecurity and psychological problems that divorces often cause the partners' children, but on some of Jesus' sayings and St Paul's writings.

Here again we have a parallel with Communist practice in Russia and Eastern Europe. Their reasons for banning all but the smallest forms of private enterprise were based entirely on a belief in the higher moral virtue of working for the community, rather than on a pragmatic assessment of the relative efficiency of the two forms of economic organisation.

Now religion is not supposed to be a specialised activity one practises on Friday, Saturday or Sunday mornings. As its etymological derivation (from Latin *religere*, meaning to bind together, to integrate) implies, it is supposed to be the *integrator* of all our knowledge and experiences of life, and the driving power behind our response to it. How can 1300, 1900 or 2600 years' old Scriptures be the immutable integrators of knowledge about life and the Universe that is being constantly expanded by pragmatic means?

The contemporary decline in Christian religious faith and practice goes well beyond those educated classes which understand the scientific method and are interested in it. Let us therefore examine the social and psychological effects of Jewish and Christian beliefs, and consider whether these effects are as desirable today as they may have been during the Victorian period.

3

The Christian Heritage

Religious beliefs and myths give us maps of the cosmos, the world we know and of human society, in both their physical and spiritual aspects. These are bound to affect our behaviour towards that environment. But as individuals, our religious beliefs are just one of many factors that influence our behaviour. Others include our genetically inherited gifts and defects; the time of year in which we were born; the love, severity or indifference of our parents; the influence of their ideas and principles and those of the school we attended; our class and educational background; the job or profession we practise.

When we look at large groups, however, especially whole nations, these extraneous factors cancel each other out. Behaviour characteristic of most members of that group can then be attributed to those cultural and religious features that all members of the group share. It is commonly accepted that there are certain dominant national characteristics which supersede differences between individuals in each nation. Americans are given to hyperbole, English people to understatement. Italians and Spaniards are emotionally extroverted and expressive, whereas Swedes and Finns are known for their introverted reserve. English people tend to be pragmatic and more tolerant of deviant behaviour that is not aggressively anti-social; French people, more intellectually argumentative;

Germans, the most conforming and law-abiding nation in Europe.

Beyond these national characteristics, are there certain cultural and behaviour patterns that are shared by those nations whose dominant religion of the last four centuries was some variety of Protestant Christianity? How do these patterns compare with those of the countries that remained predominantly Roman Catholic, and those dominated by the Orthodox Church? And how does 'Christendom' as a whole compare with Islam, India, China and the Buddhist countries of South-East Asia?

These cultural behaviour patterns very rarely express the proclaimed ideals of the dominant religion's founding prophet. That makes them all the more interesting, as much as the search for the social and psychological factors that produced these differences.

Individualism

The notion that individuals have the right to shape their own destiny as long as they don't impinge on the rights of other individuals is a product of Christian, and mainly Protestant, culture. In other parts of the world, people assert and sometimes fight for their family, tribal, communal and national identities and interests, but find it strange that individuals should wish to affirm interests separate from those of the family or tribe to which they belong. Marriages tend to be arranged by the couple's parents to cement business or property relationships; indeed this practice prevailed even in Catholic southern Europe until a generation ago.

What are the causes of this pronounced individualism in the Protestant-dominated cultures? One undoubtedly lies in Protestantism's original basis: the right of every literate individual to interpret the Bible's commands and teachings for him/herself, without deference to the (at that time) corrupt Catholic Church hierarchy. But was that the cause or the first expression of northern European individualism? Recent historical studies suggest the latter, and that both intellectual and

24

economic individualism were already growing in the high Middle Ages.

At least as important as a cause must be what literate Protestants read in the Bible, and especially the New Testament. A cardinal factor is the personality of Jesus of Nazareth, whom Christians of all denominations acknowledge as their faith's founder. Jesus was a *rebel*, who had no respect for the Jewish Temple dignitaries of his time – the rich hellenised Sadducees – and who could be quite scathing about the dogmatism and self-satisfaction of many of his fellow Pharisees. It requires little imagination to draw a close parallel between Caiaphas the High Priest and the Roman Catholic Pope or any of the lesser archbishops, bishops or Orthodox patriarchs. Jesus may even have been what he was accused of and crucified for: the leader of a band of Zealot liberation fighters against Roman rule.

It is true that since Constantine, the Catholic and Orthodox churches have done their best to sterilise Jesus' bad example by 'kicking him upstairs': interpreting his status as 'God's chosen Son' in the most naïvely literal and physical sense, which belief, until Constantine, was regarded as an Egyptian superstition. From his exalted position, therefore, he could say things to Temple and church dignitaries which no ordinary sinful mortal should be allowed to say.

Whether many practising Protestants actually believe this or not, at an unconscious level they feel Jesus to be very human and one of them. The fact that he was brought up as the son of a rich builder made the city merchant and artisan classes especially identify with him; which is why Calvinism spread among these classes throughout Europe until the Counter-Reformation reimposed Catholic conformity in southern Europe and southern Germany.

Another element encouraging the merchant and artisan classes to challenge the Catholic Church hierarchy's authority would be the Book of Genesis, in which God is described as the *Creator* of all things visible and invisible upon Earth; and that He made humankind alone in His own image. As *creative* people, the city artisans would have felt particularly close to

25

and inspired by this Creator God, a good deal closer than they would feel to the Church hierarchy, rulers and nobility (who did not make anything, but merely sat at the pinnacle of the social hierarchy, exploiting the other classes). By contrast, the Roman Catholic and Orthodox churches have always promised salvation to those who accepted their born station in life and respected their social superiors.

Inventiveness and Social Change

Protestant individualism in turn has produced a willingness, indeed – in America – an eagerness, for social, economic and technical change. This change has therefore been fastest, and produced fewest visible tensions, in the predominantly Protestant countries than elsewhere. Unless, of course, the social tensions noted above – drug abuse, increasing criminality, etc. – are precisely a pathological reaction by the least advantaged groups against changes which they cannot keep up with.

Other cultures, including the predominantly Catholic and Orthodox Christian ones, tend to prefer to preserve their traditional ways. The current wave of Islamic fundamentalism in Arab countries, Iran and Pakistan is as much an affirmation of injured cultural identity against what is perceived as Western cultural imperialism, as it is a doctrinal religious position.

This individual willingness to experiment with new ways of doing things accounts for the extraordinary technological ingenuity of the northern Europeans and overseas Europeans of the last two and a half centuries, with considerable contributions from the Jewish diaspora in their midst. At least equally important was the receptivity of the Protestant-dominated cultures to technological innovations, which produced the on-going Industrial Revolution. There had after all been inventors before the 18th century: one need only think of Leonardo da Vinci; but his and their inventions were never applied, except in the limited field of city fortifications.

26

Capital Accumulation and Capitalism

To apply most technological innovations requires not only a cultural receptivity to new ideas; it also demands in most cases a great deal of capital. The Industrial Revolution would never have taken off so fast in England and Scotland, therefore, if there had not been a fair amount of risk capital floating about, mostly accumulated by the thrifty merchant classes but also by the landowning classes through their dispossession of many of their tenant farmers and the enclosure of the common lands.

Capital accumulation has not been an exclusively Protestant and Jewish cultural feature. Organised banking started, after all, in 13th century Lombardy well before the Protestant Reformation, and spread to the other Italian city-states of the Renaissance. Many city-state patricians and ducal families started out as bankers and merchants: one need only think of the Florentine Medicis. A great deal of capital was also required to finance 15th century Portuguese and Spanish merchant venturers, whose explorations opened up Africa, South-East Asia and the Americas to European influence and then settlement.

For the rich and cultured Italian patricians of the Renaissance, however, the first call on their wealth was the building of sumptuous palaces and churches, and the patronising of great sculptors and painters. Financing overseas expeditions came well down their list of priorities; investing in new technologies even further down. The later Puritan Protestant merchant classes regarded expenditure on art as sensual and therefore sinful as well as wasteful, which is why most of their spare capital went into productive investment.

The Counter-Reformation's totalitarianism and the Inquisition drove the Protestant artisans and merchants away from the Catholic monarchies; and from the 17th century onwards capitalism flourished mainly in the Protestant-dominated cultures. Even in many predominantly Catholic countries, like France and Italy, the leading banking families are often Protestant or Jewish.

27

Aggression and Genocide

Capital accumulation is not the only fruit of the Christian and mainly Protestant heritage. The Christian European nations have also been the most successfully militarily aggressive of the whole world during the last two thousand years. European history since the fall of the Western Roman Empire is one of constant wars: first between invading tribes and indigenous inhabitants, then between feudal lords, finally between nation-states. The great merchant venturers and explorers of the last five centuries did not just discover distant overseas lands: they invariably set out to conquer them and exploit their native inhabitants.

All European nations participated in this plunder of the Americas and of Africa. But here again it is the countries of predominantly Protestant culture who were most ruthless and successful. The Spaniards and Portuguese conquered Central and South America and forcibly converted the local inhabitants to Catholicism, but left them alive to continue their own cultures under a Christianised veneer. They also initiated the slave trade from Africa to the Americas.

The more ruthless settlers of English-speaking North America and Australia killed off most of the tribal natives not just culturally but physically, leaving to the few demoralised survivors a few 'reservations'. As a result, the USA, Canada, Australia and New Zealand are countries of almost entirely European Protestant Christian culture and drive.

Europeans have not, of course, been the only aggressive militarists of recent times. The Mongols spread terror throughout Asia and Eastern Europe in the 14th century but their empire lasted only 200 years. But it is interesting that the most recent examples of mass slaughter and genocide by Asians – Pol Pot's killing of a third of the Cambodian population during his brief regime, and the excesses of the Chinese cultural revolution that are now coming to light – were committed in the name of the Communist ideology imported from Europe.

The same aggressive streak has dealt even more ruthlessly

28

with the non-human fauna and flora of the newly settled lands. The Americans decimated the roaming herds of buffalo in the 1870s and 1880s, and reduced large parts of the West and South-West of the United States to a dust bowl through over-cultivation. Now the fertile West Coast risks going the same way through over-exploitation of the water-table and the clear cutting of the old growth forests by timber companies.

Contemporary Western society is not the first in history to have been ecologically destructive. Over-cultivation probably contributed equally with climatic change to the erosion of the once fertile Sahara and Gobi deserts. But Celtic, Germanic, Native American and African tribal religions' reverence for trees and many totem animals, whom they see as imbued with divine spirit, kept their followers in balance with their environment in most parts of the world for millennia.

This over-cultivation is now spreading throughout the world. Artificial fertilisers are boosting crop yields in the short term, but at the cost of what ecological degradation in the long term? Factory farms are boosting veal and chicken production at the cost of incredible cruelty to the animals involved, and at the risk of serious disease among both the animals and their eventual human consumers: salmonella is rampant among the caged chickens, and mad cow disease among the boxed calves of factory farms.

Throughout the world, the industries created by the Protestant West's inventiveness are spewing out pollutants into the atmosphere and the oceans. Some rivers, lakes and ocean beaches are now so polluted that fish are dying and they are unsafe for humans to bathe in. Some chemical gases have cut holes in the ozone layer above the Earth, which may soon make sunbathing in summer too dangerous.

Is Christianity to Blame?

At this point I can hear my Christian readers – if I have any – protesting:

'What have these evils to do with Jesus' teachings? He advised the well-meaning rich to give all their wealth to the poor. How can you blame him for the ruthlessness of Western capitalist acquisitiveness? He transcended even his Jewish identity when he agreed to heal the centurion of the foreign occupying power, and he always referred to himself as "the Son of Man". How can you blame him for European aggression of the last two millennia, for the enslavement of the Africans and Native Latin Americans, the genocide of the Native North Americans, and the greedy over-exploitation of the Earth's resources?'

I am not blaming Jesus of Nazareth nor his teachings; but what role have these played in the formulation of most Christian doctrines since the Council of Nicaea? The only traces of his teachings in Christian church practice are the charitable foundations to help the poor and sick: from the mediaeval monasteries to the modern Salvation Army. But charity is not an exclusive feature of the Christian religion: it plays an important part also in Judaism, Islam, Hinduism and Buddhism. As I have already said: a dominant religion's social and psychological effects are rarely concomitant with its alleged founder's teachings.

It is a fact that the Christian, and especially the Protestant-dominated nations have been the most successfully aggressive peoples of recent centuries. It is a further fact that it is in predominantly Christian countries – not in Islamic or Buddhist countries, nor in India, China or Africa – that both capitalism and the Industrial Revolution first developed, and have subsequently grown fastest. We can argue about the reasons for this, and this can continue to be a fruitful field for academic research, but not about the reality of the historical events I am describing.

Patriarchal Monotheism

I will now put forward a few theories for this phenomenon; theories that are held by many Pagans, Feminists and some New Age followers, with due acknowledgement of the influence Freud, Jung, the behavioural psychologists, and the sociologists Weber and Tawney may have exercised. I offer them for testing to the academic community.

One important factor may be the all-male representation of deity in Jewish and Christian mythology. Anthropomorphic representations of boundless cosmic powers are, of course, but aids to human understanding of and communication with these powers. Theologians are the first to admit that the Creator of the Universe has no gender or sex.

Nonetheless, the choice of anthropomorphic representation has a profound psychological and emotional effect on any religion's adherents. All pre-Jewish and pre-Christian religions balanced female goddess figures with male gods in their myths, if they employed anthropomorphic representations at all (many Native North American tribes don't). Only in official exoteric Judaism and in Christianity is the deity represented anthropomorphically as all-male. Islam is also monotheist, but its taboo against any form of naturalistic representation of Allah makes his male character less pronounced, though Islamic societies are even more patriarchal than contemporary Jewish and Christian ones.

What an all-male deity representation tells the human unconscious is that only those characteristics that are more strongly developed in *men* in our society are 'in the image of God': those being all forms of *doing*, but mainly the creation of artefacts and fighting. Those aspects of life which *women* have traditionally been more interested in – relationships (with animals and plants as much as between humans), love, intuition, the life of the senses, – play no role in an all-male deity. Plastering churches with the slogan 'God is Love!' does not alter this unconscious message.

This exclusion of the feminine side of life from the Christian conception of the divine is further reinforced when the priesthood or ministry are reserved for men, as they still are in the Roman Catholic and Orthodox churches, and were until recently also in most Protestant and Jewish denominations.

If we need any further proof, consider on what secular occasions the Christian God is most commonly prayed to. In all wars between Christian countries both sides routinely ask for the Almighty's blessing on their arms and their cause. His priests are called on to bless the launching of new warships as much as of merchant ships, of bombers more frequently than of civilian airliners. But in two thousand years no one has dared ask God the Father to bless a brothel or gaming parlour: that indicates clearly where that God's values and priorities lie. Pre-Christian cultures also had tribal war gods – Aries, Mars, Thor, etc. – that were invoked in times of war, but they were balanced by peaceful fertility goddesses and gods.

This would also account for the greater aggressiveness, efficiency and material prosperity of the Protestant-dominated cultures of the last four centuries compared to those countries which remained Catholic or were forcibly reconverted to the Roman Church. Protestantism is patriarchal monotheism in its purest form, whereas the Goddess survives in Roman Catholic and Orthodox iconography as the Virgin Mary. Catholic theology sees her as the 'Mother of God' but not a Goddess; she can be *venerated* but not *worshipped*. But go and explain those differences to Italian, Greek and Spanish peasants and fishermen, or the inhabitants of the Austrian Alps who have a shrine to the Virgin at every crossroads! Psychologically if not theologically Mary is a Goddess.

Even Orthodox Judaism is less rigidly monotheistic than Protestant Christianity. In its exoteric form practised in the synagogues, it may appear as patriarchally monotheistic as Protestantism. But in the esoteric teachings, reserved for married male Jews over 30 years old, the female *Shekinah* (Wisdom) appears as Jehovah's bride, and their union is ritually celebrated by the father and mother of the family on the Sabbath night. Jewish mothers also play a leading role in

32

the home-based Jewish rituals, to balance the all-male teachings and debates in the synagogue.

Sexual Repression

In the pre-Judaic and pre-Christian polytheistic religions, certain goddesses presided over sexual attraction, sensual pleasure and fertility, and hallowed them: Aphrodite in Greece, Ishtar in Mesopotamia, Parvati in India, Freya among the Nordic peoples, Oshun among the Yoruba. The suppression of all goddess worship by the patriarchal monotheistic religions went hand in hand with a profanation and repression of sexual spontaneity and pleasure.

All three monotheistic religions reserve sexual intercourse for married couples for the procreation of children, and the choice of married partner was until recently determined by the parents on 'rational' grounds such as uniting adjacent parcels of farming land, businesses or countries (in royal families), rarely on young people's spontaneous attraction to each other.

But while patriarchal monotheistic morality is essentially the same across all three religions, it has traditionally been imposed only on women, who are supposed to remain virgins until marriage, and monogamously faithful to their husbands afterwards, so that the men may be sure of their children's paternity.

Judaism, Islam and Roman Catholicism have in different ways been much more accommodating to men's lusts. Islam allows men up to four wives, so that they should always have at least one bed partner, since wives were traditionally sexually taboo during their nine months of pregnancy and two years of lactation for their infants. In addition to the wives, men could enjoy any number of their female slaves as concubines.

Judaism abolished polygamy many centuries ago and expects married men to stay faithful to their wives, but has tolerated young unmarried men's premarital affairs or visits to brothels. This is also Roman Catholicism's position in

33

practice, since while pre-marital fornication and adultery are sins, their deleterious effects on the sinner's spiritual salvation can be washed away by confession to a priest.

Only Protestant Christianity allows no such outlets. Men as well as women are supposed to abide by monogamous rules, and have to carry around with them until they die the guilt feelings aroused by any sexual transgressions. This has made it of all the monotheistic traditions, the most sexually repressive for men and the dominantly Protestant cultures of Northern Europe and North America the most emotionally inhibited.

Redemption through Jesus Christ

Guilt can easily have a paralysing effect on the transgressor's self-confidence, driving him through self-loathing to drink or drugs. Christianity's genius has been to prevent such an effect of its stern moral code. Your sins can always be forgiven you, if you accept the belief that Jesus Christ took them upon Himself when he agreed to be crucified. The message to the sinner is always: 'Don't lose heart, keep trying to be good!'

Roman Catholic and Orthodox believers are forgiven their sins after confessing them to a priest: this makes it perhaps too easy to lapse again. Protestants are forgiven inside their own minds through a spiritual relationship to Jesus; this can more easily be doubted, and requires confirmation in the individual's ability to stick to agreed rules from then on. Hence Protestant men's greater sexual repression.

Repression and Aggression

Sexual repression among male primates produces aggression. Its evolutionary purpose was to drive younger males to challenge the dominant male's monopoly of sexual access to the tribe's females, leading to fights which ensured that only the strongest males were allowed to pass their genes on to the next generation.

In human societies, male sexual repression can be sublimated into collective military aggression against other nations,

34

scientific 'conquest of Nature' and business enterprise. This would explain why the most sexually repressed Protestant nations were the most ruthlessly aggressive and genocidal, but also the most scientifically curious, technologically inventive and commercially successful.

By contrast, the dominantly Roman Catholic and Orthodox cultures preserved vestigial reverence for the divine feminine in the Virgin Mary and female saints. Confession makes them in practice less sexually repressed, apart from celibate priests and monks. This made them militarily and commercially less successful than their Protestant neighbours but artistically and musically far more creative, since these arts express the emotional side of our lives and have been patronised among our Pagan ancestors by female goddesses or Muses.

Readers who find the connection between sexual repression, military aggressiveness and business enterprise unproven should observe their acquaintances. Don't the strongest supporters of monogamous 'family values' also generally hold right-wing views that are strongly nationalistic, and support military strength and – in America – foreign intervention? Aren't these views most widespread among professional military people and businessmen? Conversely, aren't those with a free-loving hippie or artist/bohemian life style also the gentlest, most peaceful and tolerant people, strongly supportive of peace and ecological movements? Nothing ever matches perfectly, but the broad trends should be clear.

Does Aggression Still Pay?

Genocidal policies of overseas conquest and settlement have always been immoral and criminal, but until recently they paid off. Western Europeans did successfully spread out over both Americas and Australia and the number of people of European descent throughout the world is now much greater than it could have been if all our ancestors had remained on the Old Continent. Mindless exploitation of the Earth's natural resources has also successfully raised the general standard of living for people of European descent, besides being highly profitable for the owners of mining, oil and industrial companies.

Not any longer. The invention of nuclear, bacteriological and chemical weapons during the last 50 years has made any military confrontation between industrial superpowers lethal for the whole human race, and probably for all the higher living creatures on Earth. This will be increasingly true also of the 'minor' wars in the Balkans, Asia and Africa, as modern weapon technologies spread throughout the world despite the leading powers' attempts to monopolise them.

Our technological inventiveness has also increased our industrial productivity to such an extent that for the first time in human history since the invention of agriculture, human work and effort has ceased to be the limiting factor on human prosperity. As the Club of Rome pointed out 25 years ago, we are rapidly approaching the limits of the Earth's timber and oil resources and of cultivable land, as well as of the ecosystem's capacity to recycle our industrial wastes. There is just no safe outlet for supercharged male aggression any more.

Rejection of the Patriarchal Monotheist Paradigm

We have felt this in the collective human subconscious for the last 50 years, and this has probably done as much as the invention of the contraceptive pill to cause a sea change in attitudes towards shared sexual pleasure before, in and out of marriage. As each generation since the 1960s has become less sexually repressed, it has also become less interested in military confrontation or macho foreign policies, and more interested in music, art and the environment. These are traditional feminine values: the growing equality of Western women with men thus probably owes as much if not more to men's unconscious feeling that society needs more feminine input, as to the efforts of the militant Feminists themselves.

These trends run directly counter to the Christian churches' and Jewish synagogues' traditional teachings, moral precepts and social effects. And as people cease to feel guilty about their sexual drives and activities, they also lose their sense of personal sin: which makes the doctrine of the Redemption meaningless to them.

This rather than intellectual difficulties with individual beliefs and doctrines, or any failures of presentation by priests, ministers and rabbis, is why I believe a growing number of their adherents are deserting the Christian churches and Jewish synagogues: a decline that has become especially steep since the end of World War II. They are deserting them as part of a general rejection of patriarchal hierarchical industrial society.

At the Parliament of World Religions in Chicago in late August 1993, Dr Gerald Barney, chairman of Millennium 2000, described the current population explosion in the Third World, and warned that if present trends continued the world's growing population would intersect with the maximum sustainable food resources around 2050 CE. He concluded: 'All religions should now ask themselves whether their present practice is consistent with the world's needs in the 21st century. As a committed Christian, it grieves me to say that I do not believe that Christianity – as it is currently practised – is sustainable in the 21st century!'

Filling the Vacuum

This collapse of the Jewish–Christian religious paradigm has left a spiritual vacuum in the West that consumerism cannot fill in the long term. As more and more people realise this, they search for renewed spirituality.

Some seek to shelter from present problems by returning to the past's simple certainties: they are the so-called Fundamentalists of all religions, insisting on the most literal interpretation of their sacred scriptures. Their aggressive intolerance of all those who disagree with them is a measure of the inner doubts about their beliefs that they are trying to repress: because theirs is a spiritual dead-end.

Others seek to reinterpret Christian or Jewish beliefs to bring them more into line with the age's spiritual needs. The best known among them are the late Jesuit physicist and

37

anthropologist, Pierre Teilhard de Chardin, and the former Dominican, Father Matthew Fox, founder of the Center for Creation Spirituality near San Francisco, and author of *Original Blessing* and *The Coming of the Cosmic Christ*.

Yet other adventurous spirits look for a renewed spirituality elsewhere: in the mystical East, especially India, or – like my friends and I – in Europe's own pre-Christian Pagan past. Only time will tell which of these avenues will produce the third millennium's dominant spiritual paradigm.

II

The Worship of Life

4

Experience

When Christian ministers or religious anthropologists ask us what we believe, Pagans will generally answer like the later Carl Jung: 'We don't *believe* in anything, because we *know*!' Most of our religious convictions and practice are based on personal experience, not external authority. Some are not – our widely held belief in reincarnation, for instance – but they are not compulsory.

To take a mundane example. I *believe* there is a city in north-east India called Calcutta. I have never been there so I cannot know for certain that it exists. But I have seen enough photographs and descriptions of it by visitors to believe in its existence. But I *know* London, Paris, Rome, Venice, New York, Chicago, San Francisco, Hong Kong, Manila, Singapore and Bombay and many other cities because I have visited them and know what they feel like.

A Designer Religion?

In early 1994, an article in the London *Observer*, by a Christian clergyman, called contemporary New Age spirituality with its emphasis on the primacy of personal experience a 'designer religion'. The author implied that New Agers and Pagans like a dose of spiritual uplift that is not too demanding either intellectually (no required beliefs) nor ethically (no strictures against sexual promiscuity). If that is all it was, and it had been consciously concocted for these purposes, it wouldn't work!

On the contrary, as the following testimonies show, a deity we call 'the Goddess' intervened in our lives and called us to follow Her. Like Luther before the Worms Diet, we can 'do no other'.

The Vision of Aphrodite

I was the only child of parents who divorced when I was two years old. My father did not then have the means, nor my mother the inclination to bring me up, so I was taken on by my forceful over-protective Jewish maternal grandmother. She over-fed me on cakes, so that I was always too fat to run and play with other children. At the outbreak of World War II she took me to French Switzerland, leaving her husband and my mother behind in England.

As the little fat foreigner I was naturally an outsider and inclined to introspection. From the age of 12, I went out of school hours on long solitary country walks when my contemporaries would be playing. It was on these walks, in the marvellous countryside above Lake Geneva, that I first felt a sense of oneness with the Universe, the moon and stars above, the hills and trees around me. I also felt closest to whatever power had brought all these wonders into existence, and now maintained the marvellous balance of Nature.

I never felt anything of the sort in the cold rational Protestant churches, and only a faint whiff of it in the warmer more colourful Roman Catholic ones. My grandmother never sought to indoctrinate me, except to say: 'All religious dogmas are lies!' and Goethe's dictum: 'Honour silently the ineffable!'

Christian catechism   Nonetheless, when I was 13, she sent me to Protestant catechism with the advice: 'It is part of the cultural baggage of an educated European to know who Moses, Elijah, Jesus, Paul and all that crowd were. So learn

42

what they have to teach you. As to whether you want to believe it, make up your own mind!'

The three ministers of the parish of St François in Lausanne were kind, gentle and well-meaning men, who had the best interests of their flock at heart. They were fond of me because I took their teachings seriously, unlike some of my cynical classmates. But despite their best endeavours I found the God of the Old Testament utterly repugnant.

Jesus was a much more sympathetic figure: the height of human goodness as one could imagine it! But I never could believe that he was any more divine than any other good man in history, nor grasp why his death on the cross and resurrection a day and two nights later should affect my soul's salvation one way or another. Nonetheless, at the age of 15 I wanted to belong, and so accepted to be confirmed, hoping it was enough to believe in the ethics of the living preaching Jesus to call myself a Christian.

At the confirmation ceremony, the officiating minister gave each of us a verse. Mine was: 'Jesus looked at him and loved him, and said to him: "Follow me!" ' 'Look out! That's a call to the ministry!' said one of my classmates. I could not imagine myself ever being a Christian minister, with my scepticism about some of the key beliefs. Little did I know then that I would be destined to become a priest in a quite different religion.

At 16 I returned to England and spent two years at an Anglican High Church public (i.e. private boarding) school. At the end of every Sunday service, we had to turn to the East and recite the Nicene or Apostles' Creed. I had to remain silent for the two-thirds of the Creed that I did not believe. Finally, a year later, I recognised that one cannot take a religion on a cafeteria basis. Since I did not and had never believed in the core Christian tenets, I could not honestly call myself a Christian.

First intuition From school I went straight to Cambridge, and its intense evening social life. Even then, in the late 1940s, it already had an evangelical fundamentalist society: the Cambridge Inter-Collegiate Christian Union (CICCU, pronounced 'kick you' because of their intrusive proselytising methods). Two CICCU students canvassed me, and I engaged them in theological argument. One soon gave me up as a hopeless cause, but the other kept visiting me, more to unburden his soul and share his own unhappiness than in any hope of converting me.

He must have been either sexually or emotionally abused in his younger days – or else racked by guilt at some messy sexual experience – because his misogyny was so extreme as to be laughable. In his speech and his letters to me, he said women were the root of all evil in the world. I felt sorry for him, but took the opposite side of the argument to try and broaden his mind.

One day, during a walk, I heard myself saying: 'The Christian churches keep saying that "God is Love!" So human love must be at least the reflection of divine love. What is the purest and most selfless form of love found among us? Surely, it is the love of a mother for her child, and of many a woman for her husband. Because they are more capable of loving more selflessly and more deeply than us men, surely women must be closer to God than we are!'

I surprised myself with this thought, because I had never previously thought deeply about the matter. But the Goddess heard me, and remembered.

My first love My remark about women was not at that time based on any personal experience. I had grown up well before the sexual revolution, and had attended only boys' schools. Cambridge colleges were then segregated and there were only two women's colleges compared to a dozen or more men's. So I found it difficult to understand young women and to interest them in me. I graduated at the age of 21 without ever experiencing a deep relationship. At Cambridge, however, I had managed to sublimate my frust-

44

rated sexual energy into political activism for European federalism.

The heart cannot be denied for ever, and the time came when I found sexual frustration no longer bearable. So one evening, I sank to my knees and prayed earnestly to God that He let me meet a girl whom I could love and respect, and who would love me in return. The immediate effect was a state of inner peace and confidence, as a voice in my head said: 'Have faith! She will come in due course. Meanwhile, just concentrate on your studies!'

A few weeks later, as I was preparing for a ball, I felt that that night would bring me the companion I had prayed for. Yet the evening began inauspiciously. I found myself stuck with a girl of Rubenesque proportions whose conversation was as thick as her thighs, and whom it required the dexterity of a tank commander to manoeuvre around the dance floor. At midnight, I was prepared to call it quits when a group of fellow students suddenly appeared from a private ball with some local girls in tow. One of them, Mary, was unaccompanied so I danced with her for an hour before taking her home. She was as light, graceful and witty as my previous companion had been thick. When I awoke the next day, I was madly in love. One week and three dates later, she returned my love passionately.

For the two years that our engagement lasted, we were separated most of the time by my studies, but were in constant telepathic contact. Each of us always knew what the other was feeling, and these intuitions were invariably confirmed by the next letter. On one occasion, I fell out of love for a few hours and wondered what I saw in Mary. It didn't last long before I was again feeling passionate, and I had been careful not to write to her during these few doubting hours. Yet in her next letter, she wrote: 'You have been having doubts, darling. I could feel it. Please don't make me suffer!'

When we met again during the next long vacation, it was Mary who took the initiative in making our relationship physical. I was totally unprepared and did not want to make

45

her pregnant, so I restrained myself. As she climaxed, I was suddenly catapulted out of space and time into cosmic consciousness: I was all the males of all ages and species making love to all the females of all time, while around us all the other couples were watching us like bodhisattvas in a Tibetan mandala, nodding approvingly as if to say: 'Well done! Welcome to the club!'

In my head, a gentle but strong feminine voice was saying: 'All the empires and political systems, all the dogmas, philosophies and ideologies that men have formulated since the dawn of history, put together weigh less in the divine scales than a single embrace of two young lovers, or a single smile on the lips of a new-born infant as it gazes at its mother for the first time!'

The next day, I felt in a state of pure grace, cleansed of all sin by Mary's love. I floated on Cloud Nine with Mary for ten days, but after we parted, the curse of the intellectuals reasserted itself, and I felt I had to analyse my experience. If there were divine powers, I felt I had just encountered one, but which one? Not the vengeful Jehovah of the Old Testament, nor his long-suffering crucified Son: Christianity and mystical sexual experiences just don't mix!

So I immersed myself in books on sexual psychology on the one hand, comparative religion and religious history on the other. Their insights intersected at the description of the love goddesses of Ancient Babylonia and Greece. So it was Aphrodite Herself whom I had encountered in Mary's arms! So She is a real power, not the lifeless idol described by Christian ministers. It was She who had brought me peace of mind when I prayed to God in my frustration, She who had brought Mary and me together, She who had taught us the reality of telepathy and who had finally opened my consciousness to Her cosmos during our first intimate embrace!

I did not fully share these speculations with Mary, but she sensed from my letters what was going on. She realised that marrying into her very conservative Catholic family would hinder me in my spiritual development, yet she was not prepared to break with them herself. So six weeks before our

46

planned marriage, she broke off our engagement, though it took another 12 months of deep unhappiness on both sides before our telepathic link was finally broken.

The Path to Wicca Freed from having to pretend to be Christian, I could now pursue my quest for fellow worshippers of the great Goddess in earnest. The English anthropologist Gordon Rattray Taylor's book *Sex in History* alerted me to the theory that the mediaeval witches were not a mere figment of Inquisitors' sadistic imaginations, but the survival of a country Earth Mother religion. So I started looking for books on witchcraft, and it did not take me long to find Gerald Gardner's *Witchcraft Today*. For all his presentation of witchcraft as an innocuous survival from the past, it contained enough hidden cues to ring all my spiritual bells.

So I wrote to Gerald Gardner and was invited to meet him at his London flat in Holland Park. That meeting was followed by others with the members of his first coven. During the third such meeting, Jack Bracelin, Gerald's Man Friday, told me and another candidate that we had been accepted by the coven and would be initiated at the coming February Eve festival.

When the blindfold was removed from my eyes, and I found myself in a dark incense-filled candle-lit cottage surrounded by naked figures, I felt again the presence of the same divine power whom I first encountered in Mary's arms. And when the acting High Priestess read *The Charge of the Goddess*, I felt this power welcoming me home!

Wicca has remained my spiritual home for the last 40 years and will likely continue to be for the remainder of my life. The covens to which I have belonged have been like extended families, with strong bonds of mutual affection between all members, whatever our intellectual and philosophical differences might be at times.

I had one more mystical experience – which I have already described in the first chapter – one year after my initiation and two days after my second degree elevation. But since then such dramatic experiences have not been necessary, because I am in

47

daily contact with the Goddess who has guided my life: giving me in due course a wonderful companion for 27 years, strength and consolation when that companion left me for the summerlands, a new set of friends and in due course a new companion. Through Wicca and direct inspiration I have learned to recognise Her advice in little synchronicities, and when I am too thick She sends me one of her priestesses to give me the advice directly.

The Call of Isis

The Hon. Olivia Robertson, co-founder of the Fellowship of Isis with her late brother Lawrence, Earl of Strathloch.

'My brother Lawrence, his wife Pamela and I have had mystical, spiritual and psychic experiences. These are of no value unless they are acted upon. I have had spiritual guidance and this involved acknowledging the God in men, the Goddess in women and the divine Spirit in all beings. In this shadow world of unreality, all is reflection. It is a school where we struggle to learn from our mistakes. I make about one mistake a day.

'The emphasis my brother and I lay on the Goddess is that we are entering on a new cycle of time and space in which the Divine Feminine is beginning to manifest. This Feminine is not, as many assert, Yin, Moon, inert, soft, moist and dark; while Yang is male and positive. Both Yin and Yang should be in perfect balance in each individual, but manifest variously in the Great Goddess mode or the Great God mode. Hence a man demonstrates 'Sun' and 'Moon' in one way, a woman in a different way. Power acts in polarity between Man and Woman and all generative creatures. It flows like-to-like between people of the same sex.

'The Fellowship of Isis includes all. The Goddess does not subtract: She adds! The old humanity – patriarchal, aggressive, dogmatic – can co-exist with the emerging new humanity which is rapidly developing extra-sensory powers: telepathy, bi-location, clairvoyance, clairaudience and telekinesis. My aim through the Fellowship of Isis is to bring harmony

48

between individuals and groups; religions and ways of life. Above all I wish to work with all our members in saving the Earth and all its creatures from destruction through misuse of science. I honour the Deity in all!'

Francesca De Grandis, poet, author of *Goddess Wisdom, a Celtic Shaman's Guide*, who also runs a school of Faerie magic in San Francisco:

'The college I attended had two campuses, separated by a forest. I often had to walk through those woods at night, and the path was not lit. I was terrified: I believed the Faerie folk lived in that wood, and I would run as quickly as I could, thinking they wanted to abduct me and treat me cruelly.

'Little did I know that the Fey folk are a kind race and that I was a witch with Fey blood in my veins. The Faeries in those woods must have been calling me, and I feared the call because I knew no better.

'Many years later a fortune-teller told me that my work this lifetime is to bring the Faerie magic to the human race. She told me of a lifetime long ago when I was a half-breed: half human, half magical being. I was shocked that with little knowledge of me she gave me such accurate information. Unknown to her, when I was given that psychic reading I was celebrating the fifth anniversary of my school where I teach Fey magic.

'For ten years I have run this school. Sometimes I go crazy because my blood is part Fey and I don't always know how to bring this magic to those who are more human than me. The psychic reader had summed it all up: there is a breed of witches always known to talk to the Fey folk, and to have Fey blood in their veins.

'The (Celtic) god Dagda drew a veil between humans and the Fey folk because their destinies were to be no longer intertwined. The Goddess has charged me to help bring the Fey magic back through that veil, so that we as humans can be renewed with the starry-eyed mysticism of the "little people", the passion and wisdom of the poet in love with the Goddess, and the wild integrity of the dark and dangerous Faerie folk.

'People are dying body and soul for want of the poetry of the Fey people. Faerie magic is not a poetry on the page but a living breathing poetry, the poetry of ritual, the poetry of waking each morning to the Mother's embrace, the art of walking with Her on the way to work. I try to offer my students a glimmer of that, touch their DNA with my Faerie breath so their racial memory will wake up – so that their blood will remember just a little bit how it flowed when they were Fey.

'Every day I am privileged to know that magic: the Goddess walks with me wherever I go, and I truly can feel Her presence. She is not a belief, but an actual tangible presence in my life that comforts and guides me.

'Every fall the sun turns from us, and we enter into the darker time of year. The Dark Goddess often has a much kinder face than the White Goddess. Does not the Goddess of night embrace us that we may sleep until we are healed of our cares? Yet, when winter approaches, we often do not rejoice, nor run to meet it. Darkness scares people: we fight it.

'So every fall I go into a trance and ask the Mother: "What are my plans for the season ahead? Do I need to emphasise solitude this winter? Should I go for walks on the beach nearby, where the cold grey sky can calm me? Should I focus on the company of those I love? Travel to see my family? Should I be a light in the dark, having friends gather in my home for rituals, dinners and parties? What business projects will benefit from being done in this dark time of the year? Have you plans for me other than those I might think of?" Then I listen to Her guidance, for She knows what I will need.

'Since I have started this practice of aligning myself with the seasons of the years, I have found fall and winter to be a centred rich time. Thus have my magical powers helped me enjoy abundance in the dark time which is, after all, half of every year. The one year I neglected this practice I was disoriented and very unhappy.

'Another spell helped me get over my fears of public speaking. I have hosted radio shows on major market stations, but to do so I had to overcome an enormous fear of public speaking. One of the challenges of live radio is that you've no time to decide what to say, because you can't have long silences when broadcasting. But I was terrified to start talking in front of thousands of people if I didn't know how the very sentence I was beginning was going to end.

'One day, before a broadcast, I realised that every time I started a sentence, though I was moving into unknown darkness, that darkness was my Goddess who would catch me and bring me where I needed to go. I then used my powers as a witch to visualise and actualise this all as true. I spoke that day eloquently and surely, with little fear.'

Christina Oakley, Editor of the (British) Pagan Federation's quarterly *Pagan Dawn:*
'From my early teens I felt the whole Universe to be a living system in which I belonged, and the whole of life to be sacred. I thought I was alone to have such feelings. It wasn't until I went to college that friends pointed out to me that there were others with the same feelings: they are called Pagans.'

Rhianon, a German witch living in Austria:
'I was brought up as a Roman Catholic by my parents and went to a Church school. When I was 12, I started rebelling against going to church on Sundays: I found the ritual meaningless, and an imposition on my personal freedom to be forced to attend it. When I was 14, I began to wonder why the Church called sexual feelings and enjoyment of one's body sinful, sexual activity and unmarried mothers dirty. I decided I wanted no part of a religion with such a dirty guilt-ridden attitude to natural feelings and activities.

'At first I became an atheist, but found after a while that I could not live without a religion. I felt that if anything is sacred it is life itself, so I became a pantheist. Only later did I discover that there are others who share my feeling about life; that is when I joined the Pagan movement.'

Isis, another German witch interviewed by Gisella Graichen for her book *Die neuen Hexen* (The New Witches):
'... It happened at a time when I was wholly at the end of my

tether. My children had grown up and were leaving the house, my mother had a nervous breakdown, and my marriage broke up. I had always drawn my strength until then from Christianity, from Jesus Christ's teachings to love fellow human beings and help them ... But at that point, when I felt completely broken, the Christian source of inner power no longer functioned.

'It was in that situation that I came across a group of witches with their intense conviction, that the Goddess and the God can help them to recognise their own inner strength, to develop it and to be creative as women. This was new to me, because I had been brought up with the belief that a woman has to be married to reach her full potential ... I learned from the witches to become more conscious of my femininity and to develop it independently...'

Joan, a Californian Pagan whom I met in a circle in Oakland:
'My parents were Baptists and used to take us to chapel every Sunday morning. When I was seven years old, my 10-year-old brother was diagnosed with a brain tumour and was given only a few months to live. One night I had a very vivid dream, in which I was told that if the whole of our Baptist congregation would pray for my brother, he would be healed of the tumour.

'So the next Sunday, I got up in the middle of the service to tell the congregation of my dream and ask them to pray for my brother. This interruption from a child went down very badly with the minister, who explained testily that is not the purpose of Christian prayer: we must pray to God only for the spiritual strength to accept with fortitude life's trials, not to deflect the suffering He sends us. So the congregation did not pray for my brother, who duly died a few months later.

'I decided then and there that I would have no part of such a heartless and useless religion. When I grew up, I became a Pagan when I discovered they believe in a Goddess and God who will assist in spiritual healing when invoked.'

Reformed Druids of North America

Some paths into Pagan worship are odd. In her survey of American Pagans *Drawing Down the Moon*, Margot Adler describes the beginnings of the Reformed Druids of North America (RDA) in the early 1970s. A college had the rule that all students must attend a religious service every Sunday morning, though they were free to choose the denomination to which they went. Two atheists decided to make a monkey of this role by inventing the RDA as a vehicle for Sun worship. They wrote a set of plausible rituals, and recruited a significant number of members to go up a hill and worship the sun every Sunday morning.

After a year, the college authorities capitulated and abolished the rule of compulsory Sunday morning religious attendance. Mission accomplished, the founders then moved to disband the RDA, but their members refused. They had gained considerable spiritual uplift from their weekly rituals and wished to continue these. So to its founders' disgust, the RDA has continued to be a serious Pagan religious organisation to this very day.

Trust in Personal Experience

Pagans are not just people who have had experiences of the divine. We also *trusted* these experiences more than that which older authorities were trying to teach us about life: be they priests, ministers, rabbis, or scientists in white coats. And above all, we were unable to fit those experiences into the theological or philosophical framework that these authorities were offering us: in my case, because my experience of the divine came through an activity that the Christian churches condemn as sinful indulgence.

When I told a fellow student of my telepathic contact with my distant fiancée, he said it was impossible: experiments conducted by Dr Rhine in Oxford and the US Navy had shown mind to mind transmission of card images did not achieve a hit rate much greater than pure guesswork. I don't know whether this is an accurate description of Dr Rhine's and the US Navy's results, but I regarded it as totally irrelevant to my own experience. My fiancée and I were experiencing tele*pathy*, which means transmission of *feelings*. What Dr Rhine and the US Navy were attempting was transmission of *abstract images* which should properly be called tele*logy*. But even if the experiments had been concerned with telepathy, I would not have let a failed scientific experiment undermine my confidence in my own experience.

Years later, I described my two mystical experiences to a prominent Mensa member. 'Oh!', he said, 'I have had such an experience in a very vivid dream. But if I had given any credence to it, I would have had to alter my whole [materialist scientific] outlook on life, which would have robbed me of my intellectual security. So I thought it safer to attribute it to the amount of cheese I had eaten just before going to bed!'

Christian Mystical Experiences

Pagans are not alone in having sometimes overwhelming religious or mystical experiences. 'Born-again Christians' who re-enter the Church after years of agnosticism or indifference are usually impelled to do so by a sudden experience in which they 'meet Christ', or by the fulfilment of a prayer they uttered at a moment of personal crisis, like the one that led to my meeting Mary.

At a joint meeting between a Pagan discussion group and a Christian Evangelical group, several Evangelicals described experiences while walking in the country in which they suddenly felt themselves totally at one with life. These experiences confirmed their belief that a loving God is at the heart of the Universe, and they felt they had just 'met Christ'.

To the born-again Christian, however, the personal experience that leads him back into his Church is the only one he is allowed to trust. Once back in his congregation, he is expected to 'have faith' in the external authority of the Bible or – if he is Roman Catholic or Orthodox – the Church on all spiritual and moral matters.

In my second year of catechism classes in Lausanne in 1946, the minister once asked us why we thought people no longer had the direct revelations of God that the Apostles had in the years following Christ's crucifixion. He answered that God no longer needed to communicate in this manner now that He has established the channel of the Scriptures (a Roman Catholic priest would have said the Church) to communicate His teachings.

But many people do have mystical experiences at critical points in their life and have had in every century of the last two millennia. What the minister was telling us – though he probably didn't realise it – is that if any of us should have a mystical experience, we should not trust it but discuss it with our minister.

In an otherwise very fair and balanced discussion of the resurgence of witchcraft, a German Lutheran theologian admits that mystical experiences do occur, but warns readers that the powers one encounters in such experiences can as easily be demonic as angelic. The mystic should therefore seek guidance from his pastor or priests. In other words: when a mystical experience confirms Christian teaching or can be fitted into it, it is harmless but redundant; but when it defies it, as my experience in Mary's arms did, it is to be rejected as 'demonic'.

New Age and Eastern Spiritual Paths

Christians are not alone in being told to look outside themselves to external authorities for spiritual guidance. This is also true not just of the other scriptural religions – Judaism and Islam – but of many branches of New Age thinking, an umbrella concept that is often used to cover all the new religious movements, including Paganism.

Among them, those who specifically call themselves New Age often take the late Alice Bailey's writings as authoritative. The Anthroposophists, a Gnostic Christian movement founded by the Austrian mystic Rudolf Steiner, frequently take his writings as the last word on any subject he wrote about:

metaphysics and philosophy, biology, architecture, education. This despite the fact that Steiner put most of his ideas forward as hypotheses, and told his followers to prove all things for themselves.

Eastern gurus are notoriously authoritarian. Swami Prabhupada's word is law in the International Society of Krishna Consciousness which he founded, as is that of the Rev Sun Myung Moon in the Unification Church.

Of all the Indian gurus, the one whose teachings came closest to contemporary Western Paganism was the late Bhagwan Shree Rajneesh. His philosophical lectures are indeed delightful for their humour and outrageous insights, but he found it impossible – assuming he tried – to wean his followers from dependence on him, and to move from seeing the divine in him to discovering it within themselves. Before his death, Osho (Hindi for 'Grandpa') installed a medium to be his successor at the head of the Puna ashram, through whom he hoped to continue guiding his followers from the other side.

The Primacy of Personal Experience

Pagans have no such problems. We have no required beliefs that might conflict with any mystical experiences we might have, nor with our everyday experience of the world, nor with new scientific discoveries about the origin of the Universe. As Margot Adler put in *Drawing Down the Moon*: 'In Paganism and witchcraft, no one ever asked me to believe anything!' We may, of course, influence each other subconsciously in our social contacts in adopting beliefs that do not contradict our personal experiences but are not based on them either: reincarnation is a case in point. T. M. Luhrmann has called this 'interpretive drift', in her seminal work *Persuasions of the Witch's Craft*.

Paganism is a religion of experience, not belief: not just prior to joining, but as part of the very fabric of collective religious practice. It is thus adaptable to any social or ecological environment, and encourages open-minded curiosity about all natural phenomena that meshes perfectly with the best of contemporary science. We only reject the dogmatism of *materialist scientism*, which asserts that only the external 'objective' perceptions of our five senses have any reality, and that 'subjective' inner experiences must be discounted as 'unreal' and 'irrational'.

Why Organise Paganism?

Given the extreme individualism of Pagans, and our rejection of all outside authorities, how can we agree on enough to organise ourselves into covens, groves, nests, gatherings and formal Federations? And why should we want to?

Because Pagans, like all human beings, are social animals and some of us like to share the convictions that mean most to us with those of like mind. Sharing our convictions in organised rituals reinforces them in our minds, as the rituals of all religions do for those who practise them. But there also many Pagans who are happy to worship and develop spiritually on their own.

We have enough to celebrate in common because marvelling at and revering Life in all its complexity and feeling part of it is the natural religious attitude of people who have not been heavily indoctrinated otherwise. It is an attitude shared not only by all the strands of contemporary Paganism but by Taoism, Tantric Hinduism and tribal peoples all over the world.

It was the same with the Protestants 475 years ago. Against the Church's pretensions to interpret the Scriptures for them, they affirmed the right of every literate individual to read the Bible for him/herself and to interpret it accordingly. But those who came to similar conclusions in their interpretation still banded together in Lutheran, Calvinist, Zwinglite, Presbyterian, Congregational churches and in the Society of Friends.

Pagan individualism and covening is the natural outgrowth of four and a half centuries of Protestant individualism, and it is significant that it is growing mainly in the countries of Protestant culture: the English-speaking countries throughout the world, and more recently also northern Germany, The

Netherlands, Norway, Sweden and Finland. There is little Neo-Paganism in the Roman Catholic countries of southern Europe, where they still observe many old Pagan customs under a Catholic veneer: as do the Latin American followers of Santeria, Voudun, Candomble and Macumba, syncretistic religions combining Catholic saint veneration with Yoruba *orisha* invocation.

5

The Goddess

Who is this Goddess who manifested spontaneously in my and many other Pagans' lives? She is the Supreme *Being* (as distinct from the Supreme *Creator* or *Doer*), the sum total of all the energy and matter in the Universe, which She keeps integrated harmoniously by the power of Love in all its aspects:

- our attachment to our environment as it is ('I love my valley!'),
- the sexual drive that perpetuates life ('I love my wife and children'),
- the food chain ('I love roast beef!').

She is immanent in the eternal life cycle of all creatures, animals, plants, rocks and winds as much as of humans: their Mother and nurturer when they are born, their Lover and companion when they have matured, and their Death in old age or when they are killed and devoured by a predator. She then welcomes them to the spirit world for a period of restful amnesia before being reborn. But She can also be awesomely fierce in Her destruction of all impurities, be it on the surface of the Earth or in Her worshippers' lives.

Pagans often refer to Her as the Triple Goddess and her three aspects are equated to the three visible phases of the

Moon: the waxing crescent as Maiden and Lover, the full moon as Mother, the waning crescent as the Crone goddess of old age and death. These three aspects are often described as distinct goddesses in the ancient Pagan mythologies: Kore or Aphrodite, Demeter and Hecate/Persephone in Greek myth; Rhianon, Brighd and Cerridwen among the Celts; Parvati, Lakshmi and Kali among the Hindus.

But the Goddess is not just the Moon. Like the Egyptian goddess Nut She is also the whole of the night sky; and She is Gaia, the Earth Spirit and the life cycle of all living creatures on Earth. She is eternal as the ever present which alone is real: the past being no more than the phantom of our memories, and the future a figment of our imaginations. A Pagan song expresses our relationship to Her as individuals:

We all come from the Goddess, and to Her we shall return, like a drop of rain flowing to the ocean!

Although the Goddess is ever present in all our lives, we are most aware of Her when we live most intensely and are aware of doing so. She will appear to us as a gorgeous Alpine or Himalayan sunset after an exhausting but exhilarating mountain climb; in the rhythms of a wild dance; in a tasty and lovingly cooked meal enjoyed in convivial company. But we come closest of all to Her in the passionate ecstasy of physical love; in the painful muscular contractions that bring a new life into the world; and when we hold a loved one in our arms as (s)he breathes her or his last!

Why anthropomorphise Her then, instead of simply calling Her the Life-Force? As an aid to human understanding, and to emphasise the fact that for all Her boundless universality and eternity, it is possible to enter into a personal relationship with Her. Not all Pagans personalise Her in this way, however; many would just say that they 'worship Nature.'

The Manifestation of Isis

The feelings of those who relate to a personal Goddess are best expressed in this part of Lucius Apuleius' third century novel *The Golden Ass*, taken from the 1951 Robert Graves translation:

'When I had finished my prayer and poured out the full bitterness of my oppressed heart, I returned to my sandy hollow, where once more sleep overcame me. I had scarcely closed my eyes before the apparition of a woman began to rise from the middle of the sea with so lovely a face that the gods themselves would have fallen down in adoration of it. First the head, then the whole shining body gradually emerged and stood before me poised on the surface of the waves. Yes, I will try to describe this transcendental vision, for though human speech is poor and limited, the Goddess Herself will perhaps inspire me with poetic imagery sufficient to convey some slight inkling of what I saw.

'Her long thick hair fell in tapering ringlets on her lovely neck, and was crowned with an intricate chaplet in which was woven every kind of flower. Just above her brow shone a round disc, like a mirror, or like the bright face of the moon, which told me who She was...

'All the perfumes of Arabia floated into my nostrils as the Goddess deigned to address me: "You see me here, Lucius, in answer to your prayer. I am Nature, the universal Mother, mistress of all the elements, primordial child of time, sovereign of all things spiritual, queen of the dead, queen also of the immortals, the single manifestation of all the gods and goddesses that are. My nod governs the shining heights of Heaven, the wholesome sea-breezes, the lamentable silences of the world below. Though I am worshipped in many aspects, known by countless names, and propitiated with all manner of different rites, yet the whole round earth venerates me.

'"The primeval Phrygians call me Pessinuntica, Mother of the gods; the Athenians, sprung from their own soil, call me Cecropian Artemis; for the islanders of Cyprus I am Paphian Aphrodite; for the archers of Crete I am Dictynna; for the trilingual Sicilians, Stygian Proserpine; and for the Eleusinians their ancient Mother of the Corn.

'"Some know me as Juno, some as Bellona of the Battles; others as Hecate, others again as Rhamnubia, but both races of Æthopians, whose lands the morning sun first shines upon, and the Egyptians who excel in ancient learning and worship me with ceremonies proper to my godhead, call me by my true name, namely, Queen Isis.

'"I have come in pity of your plight, I have come to favour and aid you. Weep no more, lament no longer: the hour of deliverance, shone over by my watchful light, is at hand."'

An inner vision, like mine in the arms of my first fiancée. But it also expresses one of the key differences between Pagan and Christian visions of the divine. To us, the Goddess is not only loving and compassionate, as Christians perceive Jesus Christ to be, but physically shiningly beautiful!

Pantheism and Monism

Most branches of contemporary Paganism share this pantheistic concept of divinity. We see it as being not just immanent in all parts of the visible and invisible world, but coterminous with them: the spirits as well as the bodies of all human beings – female as well as male – animals, plants and even rocks, as well as the planets and stars above the Earth. We fully accept the saying attributed to Hermes Trismegistus:

That which is below is as that which is above,
And that which is above is as that which is below,
But according to a different manner.

In other words: If you want to understand the cosmos, study the human soul. If you want to understand the human soul study the cosmos.

This is in strict contrast to the Judeo-Christian tradition of seeing the One and Only Creator God as *transcendent*, i.e. separate from His creation, and so remote from it that He only truly incarnated once (according to Christians) in the person of the historical Jesus of Nazareth.

Of course, nothing is ever wholly black and white, least of all in theology. There is also an immanent element in the Christian God, in the third person of the Trinity – the Holy Ghost or Spirit – who is believed to descend at baptism into the soul of Christians and then informs their conscience.

Similarly, there is also a transcendent side to Pagan deities, since they are to be found not only within our souls but in those of other people, in the animals, plants and Earth around us, in the spiritual as well as the physical world, and thus also outside ourselves as individuals. Nonetheless, Paganism puts the emphasis on the immanence of the divine in the whole of Creation, which we see as inherent and not conferred by a selective sacrament such as the Christian baptism.

Unlike Jews, Unitarians and Humanists, Pagans thus have no difficulty in accepting that Jesus of Nazareth was God incarnate. Where we differ from Christians is that we do not accept the implied non-divinity of all other human and living beings.

Contemporary Paganism is also monistic in that we see the divine equally in the spiritual world and the physical creation, and therefore our bodies and all their functions, but especially in the physical expression of sexual love. And most importantly we see the divine incarnate in women and the females of all species as much as in men.

This contrasts with Judaeo-Christian dualism, which pits the Spirit (mostly confused with the intellect) against the Flesh (which includes all our instinctual drives), and sees the former alone as made in 'God's image', and our souls as exiled in our physical bodies. This is based on the Book of Genesis, in which God made 'humankind alone in His image'. The only thing that therefore expresses God's nature is the feature that human beings alone possess (to the best of our knowledge) of all beings on Earth: our ability to self-reflect and to create intellectual abstractions. And since women have until now generally appeared less interested in these than men, this is held in turn to justify their subservience to men and their exclusion from the priesthood in patriarchal societies.

63

Immanence and Quantum Physics

The Pagan assertion of the divine nature of life itself is shared by Chinese Taoism, the Shaivate-Shaktiite-Tantric branch of Hinduism, and most tribal religions. Nor does its validation lie solely in direct mystical experiences, whether spontaneous or induced by meditation or magical ritual. It is the religious concept that harmonises best with modern quantum physics.

This has discovered that all forms of matter and of life are composed of atoms of varying degrees of density caused by the varying speed at which their elementary particles fly around the nucleus. Matter is thus suspended energy, and can be turned back into energy, as the inventors of wood- and coal-burning furnaces, steam engines and the internal combustion engine already knew two centuries before our physicists first split the atom.

Human thoughts, including those which have preceded the composition of this page, are low-voltage currents that fire neurons inside our brains. Thus our minds like our bodies are energy at varying degrees of density and velocity. Jewish and Christian dualists find this a depressing picture. 'Do you mean to say that our highest religious insights, our deepest philosophical speculations, our finest poetic and loving feelings are *nothing but* electric currents?'

We Pagans see things differently. Far from feeling degraded to the level of 'unconscious' electricity, we see quantum physics confirming the monist view that we have always held: the whole universe is alive and *conscious*; and every animal, plant, stone, drop of water, cloud and wind has as much potential consciousness and feeling as we do, albeit at a different frequency.

This means that, given enough training in psychic awareness, each of us can communicate feelings to the animals, plants, stones, streams, lakes, seas, clouds and winds we encounter, and draw from them, as much as from our fellow human beings, the psychic energy we may need to do our everyday work or to cope with a sudden crisis. We may also influence them and events with the power of our focused minds when the need arises, which is the theoretical basis for the practice of instrumental magic, described in a later chapter.

As we do so we identify less with our mortal time- and space-bound egos and more with the eternal life-stream, and become aware that we are not alone in the Universe, and that at the deepest level of our self-awareness, as of our constituent atoms, we are immortal!

Immanence and Evolution

Even before 20th-century physicists refined quantum theory, Charles Darwin had demonstrated that the evolution of life on Earth is an immanent process. The wonderful diversity of animal and plant species – which we are unfortunately reducing sharply in our blind exploitative greed – did not appear out of nothing in 4004 BCE. The various species evolved slowly in response to environmental challenges and opportunities over millions of years from common ancestors going back to the first amoeba in tropical waters. This evolutionary process is re-enacted in the growth of every foetus in its mother's womb or – for other species – fertilised egg.

Pragmatism and Ecological Awareness

This immanent view of the divine has certain consequences. The first and foremost is that Pagans view Nature Herself as the source of any knowledge we may wish to acquire about the powers that rule our lives and the cosmos. Ours is thus a pragmatic religion, whose intense curiosity about natural processes parallels and harmonises with that of the physical sciences. I know at least two high-powered physicists among fellow Pagans, one of whom works for NASA.

Our only difference from run-of-the-mill scientists is that we do not subscribe to dogmatic materialism. We do not confine ourselves to our five senses to study nature from the outside, but seek also to communicate with all things through psychic awareness of vibrations from inside the life-stream: this is the main purpose of the initiatory magical and Wiccan orders.

Tribal people have this ability to communicate psychically with animals, plants and even stones. Religious anthropologists call this animism and have long regarded it as a primitive superstition. It shows on the contrary a greater psychic sensitivity to the world around us, which we in the 'advanced' industrial world have unfortunately repressed. We must now regain it in order to enjoy our wonderful vibrant alive world to the full.

The ancient Egyptians frequently portrayed their gods and goddesses with the bodies or at least the heads of animals, to emphasise that the divine power of life and consciousness is incarnate as much in animals as in human beings, and that we have as much to learn about life and the deities that preside over it by observing our household cats, cows and scarabs, as our fellow human beings.

Our ability to see the divine manifested in animals, trees, plants, grass and the very rocks themselves tends to make Pagans much more ecologically aware, more conservative about our natural environments, and more appalled at the mindless destruction of primal rainforests and the pollution of our environment by contemporary industry than the general public. We thus consider our religion to be not just that best suited to our own spiritual needs, but also the most relevant to the problems that contemporary society has to face.

Immanence and Equality

The Judeo-Christian transcendental view of deity leads naturally to scripture-based beliefs and a hierarchical church organisation. If one's God is so remote that He incarnated only once in the whole of human history and communicates directly only with a few chosen prophets, then knowledge about him can only be gained by listening to the priests who have been anointed by the successors of the Only Son's apostles, or the ministers or rabbis who have made a career of studying the prophets' writings.

In contrast, Pagans see all living beings as equal in their inherent divinity. The God or Goddess within can, if they want to, speak directly to anyone, Pagan or not, initiated into one of the mystery traditions like Wicca, or not, and they frequently do. It is in such direct mystical *experiences*, as described in the previous chapter, that we learned of the Goddess' *immanence*. And it is because we have experienced the Goddess as immanent in ourselves that we trust these mystical experiences to guide us in our view of the Universe.

Unlike Catholic priests, the leaders and members of Pagan covens, groves or nests have no need of any Apostolic Succession from pre-Christian Druids or mediaeval witches. The precise date to which the various Pagan traditions can trace their descent may thus fascinate a small number of would-be Pagan historians, but does not affect our ability to contact the Goddess and God within, which most Pagan groups use to judge themselves and each other.

Having said this, it would of course be boring if every individual Pagan had to reinvent the wheel each time and discover for her or himself through lengthy trial and error how to contact her or his higher self. Not everyone has the gift for, or the accumulated pressure of frustration or loneliness leading to a spontaneous mystical experience. Thus, other things being equal, a Pagan learning from a more experienced Pagan, who may or not be a Wiccan or Druid initiate, is likely to progress faster in her or his knowledge of the inner planes and in the development of her or his psychic powers than a solo experimenter with nothing but a book as guide. Some Pagan traditions use a formal initiation to 'plug' new members into the Goddess or God 'current' with which the tradition feels itself to be in contact.

However, the status of teacher in the Pagan mysteries will always be different from that of a Roman Catholic or Orthodox priest, an adept in the (Gnostic Christian) Western Mysteries, or of a Hindu or Buddhist guru. S/he will be just that: a *teacher* of spiritual techniques for self-discovery, never a 'master' or 'mistress' to whom the pupil has to surrender all her or his independent moral judgement. Any Pagan teacher who claims greater powers than this is always treated with suspicion.

The Feminist Goddess

In the 1970s the religious wing of the feminist movement discovered the Goddess and adopted Her as a 'figure of empowerment for women'. This She is indeed, but She is also much more than that. The use of this expression by some feminist writers makes one wonder how much of a spiritual reality She is to them as distinct from a symbolic convenience. Many other feminists are, however, also Pagan in their awareness and acknowledge the Goddess as a personal spiritual reality.

Since militant feminists were at that time both more numerous and more vociferous than Pagans, the Goddess has come to be seen by many theologians and most publishers as an aspect of 'women's spirituality'. This is to restrict Her far too much: as the experiences described in the last chapter show, She is a real cosmic power who can manifest in men's as much as women's lives.

Some feminists with a Christian background took over Christian theology wholesale, substituting 'God the Mother' for God the Father, and reciting the 'Lady's Prayer': 'Our *Mother* Who Art in Heaven...' To accommodate them the (Calvinist) Church of Scotland and some Methodists now refer to 'God the Father/Mother', thus seeking to maintain a now gender-neutral monotheism.

Pagans call this 'Jehovah in skirts'. We doubt whether the feminists who worship 'Her' have really studied the Bible, especially the Old Testament, and thought it through. They may proudly proclaim the Creator of the Universe as a feminine deity; but do they really want to appropriate a god who through the mouths of Moses, Joshua and later Samuel told the Israelites to kill *all* the inhabitants of the fertile Canaan lands that they coveted, not just the fighting men (as all fighting tribes did in those days), but women, children and sheep?

68

Gender metaphors

If one believes, as most Pagans do, that the leading deities are cosmic energies that predated the human race and our fertile theological imaginations, then one cannot attribute any gender arbitrarily to any deity. For the gender metaphor to have any meaning, the energy represented by the god or goddess image must manifest more strongly in the gender that represents it.

From that point of view, the energy represented by the JHVH of the Old Testament is unquestionably male: whether as the separator of the stars and planets from the space between them, and of water from earth and air on Earth; as the embodiment of Israelite tribal identity; as lawgiver to the Israelites; or – occasionally – as the giver of ruthless genocidal orders.

For several generations, Christians – especially Protestants – have found JHVH's ruthless qualities, as described in the Old Testament, profoundly embarrassing and have tried to reprogram Him as 'God is Love'. With singularly little effect on the collective behaviour of Christian and especially Protestant dominated societies. Because their imagery was all wrong! They tried portraying two *male* deities – God the Father, and His Son Jesus Christ – as symbols of *love*, whereas most people experience love as primarily a feminine attribute, and one that only women and children can evoke in most men.

The Pagan choice of a feminine image for the Life-Force is taken because Her attributes manifest much more strongly in the average woman than the average man: *unconditional love* for all creatures, including ourselves, and the whole living environment and Universe, which may also be expressed at times as ruthless *emotional fierceness* in their defence, a *cyclical* manifestation and – above all – *Being* rather than *doing*.

That is probably also why the common people of Mediterranean countries pray much more to Mary than to Jesus or God the Father when they need help in their daily lives. And that is why the Life-Force and power of Divine Love appeared as a shiningly beautiful woman not just to Lucius Apuleius, myself and countless other contemporary Pagans, but also to Catholic adolescents at Lourdes, Fatima, the rue des Saint-Pères in Paris, and most recently at Medzugorje in Croatia.

6

The Horned God

Very few Pagans want to replace the patriarchal monotheism of the last five to 2,500 years by a Goddess-oriented monotheism. Those aspects of character that manifest most strongly in the average man (though not exclusively so), a sense of identity, intellectual creativity and willpower, are as much a manifestation of divine universal powers as the Goddess' qualities of being, cyclicity and love.

The Father God of Creation

The Fellowship of Isis recognises this and has syncretised the worship of the Goddess that it promotes with that of the Jewish-Christian Father God. As Olivia Robertson, its co-founder, expressed it in a previous chapter:

'The Fellowship of Isis includes all. The Goddess does not subtract: She adds! The old humanity – patriarchal, aggressive, dogmatic – can co-exist with the emerging new humanity which is rapidly developing extra-sensory powers: telepathy, bi-location, clairvoyance, clairaudience and telekinesis. My aim through the Fellowship of Isis is to bring harmony between individuals and groups; religions and ways of life. Above all I wish to work with all our members in saving the Earth and all its creatures from destruction through misuse of science. I honour the Deity in all!'

This is also the position of the new Jewish Pagan movement in the United States. This has been founded by Pagans of ethnic Jewish descent to worship the Goddess without denying their cultural heritage. They have found the answer not in denying JHVH but in restoring to Him His ethnic bride, the Semitic goddess Asherah, who was worshipped in Canaanite temples side by side with JHVH before the days of Jeremiah and the exile in Babylon, from which the Jewish elders returned imbued with Zoroastrian monotheism.

Most other contemporary Pagans have, however, refused to recognise the Jewish-Christian God JHVH. Feeling that our own pantheistic Nature worship is a return to older pre-Christian religious traditions, they refuse to define our religion in relation to the 'upstart' and usurping Jewish-Christian patriarchal monotheistic paradigm. Like the Bad Fairy in Cinderella, JHVH is thus the uninvited guest at most Pagan theological feasts.

Those Pagans who have rebelled against a Protestant Christian or Jewish education, or who have otherwise studied the Old Testament, tend to find JHVH a repulsive figure in his jealousy of all other gods and goddesses, the joylessness of His worship, his occasional genocidal commands to the Israelites as they conquered Canaanite cities and tribes, and His twisted values that allow Him to send His 'only' Son to die a painful death to redeem human sins but not to forgive humanity outright. But since contemporary Paganism is not a dualist religion and does not, therefore, believe in a cosmic power of Evil, there is no devil position that JHVH could occupy in our theology.

Many Pagans who have thought about the matter tend, therefore, to attribute JHVH's negative features to Moses' political machinations, to the later Jewish prophets and the Christian church theologians who claimed to bring JHVH's message to the world, and refuse to contemplate the possibility that He might be a real cosmic power in His own right.

Personally, I don't think that this is a tenable position in the long run, if only because it greatly underestimates the spiritual force we are up against as we struggle to re-attune humanity with Nature. Right now, however, it is understandable. The Pagan community does not live in isolation but in the midst of a complex industrial society which – though largely de-Christianised at least in Europe – is still imbued with patriarchal values. To try and re-establish a greater psychological balance in society, we have to put all our weight on the seesaw's opposite end: in affirming our Goddess as the embodiment of Nature and of gentler more caring values. Coming to terms with the JHVH energy and relating it to our Goddess and Horned God energies can be left to a later generation.

The Horned God

Those Pagans who like to personify the Life-Force and refuse to recognise JHVH therefore give the Goddess a different consort: the Horned God, whom the Greeks called Pan and the Celts, Cernunnos. With his rutting stag or ram antlers and cloven goat's feet, He represents both assertiveness and the male aspect of fertility, sometimes even unbridled male lust, which Pagans do not see as evil or degraded, as long as it is honest in its intent and accepts 'No' for an answer. Like the Hindu god Shiva, He is also the Lord of the Dance and is often represented with a flute.

He is certainly the male equivalent of the lover and seducer aspect of Goddess, so that women have as much of a seducing deity to relate to as men. He is also a role model for Pagan men in their relations with women: both wild and therefore imaginative, like Robert Bly's *wild man*, and gentle and considerate in his love-making and later sharing in the task of nurturing children.

Yet the Horned God is far from being an artificial thought-form constructed by some contemporary Pagans. He is a distinct energy that has also manifested already in the lives of a number of Christians. The theologian Sam Keen wrote *To a Dancing God* in 1970, and the most beautiful expression of the Horned God's energy that I have read comes from a Catholic nun:

73

To Pray

by Sister Marie-Pierre

Tell them
what the wind tells the rocks,
what the sea tells the mountains.
Tell them that an immense love
pervades the Universe.
Tell them that God
is not what they believe:
that He is a wine one drinks,
        a shared feast
where everyone gives and receives.

Tell them He is
the flute player in the midnight light;
He approaches and runs away,
leaping towards the wells.
Tell them about His innocent face,
His light, shadow and laughter.

Tell them He is
your space and your night,
your wound and your joy.
But tell them also
that He isn't what you say
and that you really don't know Him at all.

Like the Goddess, the Horned God is immanent in Nature, and especially in wild animals and elemental spirits. Never very interested in sharp abstract definitions, Pagans are unclear whether the Horned God is just the male aspect of the Goddess and represents essentially the same universal Life-Force, or is a distinct complementary energy to Hers in Nature as much as in the human collective unconscious.

Those who see Him as distinct would have Him represent

the sense of identity of individual animal and plant species, and ultimately of human individuals, whereas the Goddess represents the Life-Force and all the living experiences we share with the whole of life: being born, being alive, loving, reproducing ourselves, dying. As the Lord of the Hunt, the Horned God is also the husband and father as provider, who 'brings home the bacon'.

In Wiccan teaching, both the Goddess and the Horned God are different facets of an original One: the Ancient Providence, who was from the Beginning and shall be until all Eternity, all-seeing, all-knowing, all-compassionate. But we do not think that we can comprehend it apart from mystical experiences like the one described in the first chapter.

The Faery tradition, to which the Pagan author Starhawk belongs, as well as Crowley's *Book of the Law*, see the original One splitting Itself into two – the Goddess and the Horned God – to bring the Universe and all its distinct stars, planets and life-forms into manifestation, but this is not a concept shared by all Pagans.

The Horned God's greater sense of identity has also produced some additional male gods in some contemporary Pagan traditions, quite apart from the ethnic deities I shall consider in the next chapter.

The Lord of Death and Resurrection

One old English Pagan tradition sees two vegetation kings fighting for the hand of the Earth Goddess: the Holly King and the Oak King. Every spring the Oak King defeats the Holly King: in the autumn, the Holly King triumphs. The Wiccans have taken this up and given the Goddess a winter consort distinct from the spring and summer Horned God: the Lord of Death and Resurrection.

This is largely based on the Greek Persephone myth, which is believed to have played the central role in the Eleusinian mysteries. This relates how the Maiden Goddess Kore, daughter of the Earth Mother Demeter, was snatched by Hades, the Lord of the Underworld, while she was out picking flowers and taken into the underworld to be his consort. Her mother was so distraught that She let all the plants wither until Her daughter was returned to Her. The Father God Zeus patched up a compromise whereby Kore would be with Her mother for half the year, allowing vegetation to bloom each summer, but would return as Persephone to be Hades' consort in the underworld for the winter months.

Wiccans find this myth particularly meaningful and enact it at their second degree initiations. The Lord of Death and Resurrection thus represents one of the poles between which the cyclical Life-Force alternates, including our own lives as individuals. It implies a transmigration of souls and reincarnation after a period of restful oblivion in the underworld, a belief widely held among contemporary Pagans though not required.

But is the Lord of Death and Resurrection a distinct divine energy from the Horned God, or just one of His aspects? Wiccans would be hard put to say. After all, while stags and rams rut in the springtime, thus making the Horned God a fertility figure, he is also Lord of the Hunt, which in ancient times took place mainly in the winter, both to cull the herds of deer that might have outgrown their sources of food, and to feed the village when the previous summer's and autumn's crops had become exhausted. And what is a Lord of the Hunt but the Lord of Death to the animals being hunted?

In yet another Wiccan mythical cycle, the Goddess rules over the land between the spring and autumn equinoxes, or between Beltane and Hallow'een, and the Horned God over the winter months. This would equate the Horned God quite clearly with the Lord of Death and Resurrection.

The Sun God

The Pagan Druid orders (not all Druid orders are Pagans, nor even religious) add yet another deity: the Sun, the prime focus of their religious ceremonies though they do not necessarily personify Him. This makes sense since the Sun is the dialectical

76

complement both of the Earth and the Moon, both of which symbolise the Goddess.

This makes feminists and many Wiccan Pagans suspicious. Since the Moon reflects sunlight, making the Sun the Male God and the Moon the Goddess seems to them to reaffirm subtly male primacy. They point out that in the Germanic, Baltic and Japanese languages – and the Pagan myths from these countries – the Sun is feminine and a Goddess while the Moon is masculine and a God. It would have been so with our Saxon ancestors too: hence the many tales of the 'Man in the Moon'.

Freya Aswynn, the leading European exponent of the Northern Asatru religious tradition, offers an interesting explanation for this reversal of genders of the Sun and Moon between the Latin Mediterranean and the northern Germanic and Baltic cultures. In the colder northern European climates, the Sun's warmth is gentle and nurturing and is thus perceived as a loving feminine power. The Moon, on the other hand, appears during the cold and frosty winter nights which could be deadly to anyone caught without shelter and warmth.

In the hot Mediterranean and tropical climates, on the other hand, the Sun's heat is fierce and can be deadly to anyone without proper clothing and shelter at the height of noon: he is thus perceived as a male deity. It is on the contrary the cool nights when the Moon shines which are perceived as gentle, nurturing and therefore the domain of a feminine Goddess.

The common elements of all these traditions is that the gentle and nurturing times of the day or night are perceived as feminine, the fierce and deadly extremes of cold or heat as masculine.

If Pagans are so ready to embrace often contradictory myths about our deities, it is because we do not see these myths as factual but as poetic allegories pointing to deeper truths. What they all have in common is the pantheistic conviction of the whole universe in all its diversity as being divine: the Sun, the Moon, the stars and planets as much as the Earth and its seas, rocks, plants and animals. We have something to learn from all of them, not just about our relationship to our environment but also about ourselves.

7

Ethnic Gods and Goddesses

When Pagans first discover the divine feminine in Nature, women and themselves, they call it the Goddess. Later, when they pray to or invoke Her, singly or as members of a Wiccan coven, Druid grove or other Pagan group, they find this name too impersonal and try one or more of the ethnic names by which She was known in antiquity. The most popular names are the Egyptian Isis, and the Celtic Brighd and Cerridwen. Similarly, the Horned God would be addressed as Pan or Cernunnos, the Lord of Death and Resurrection as Osiris or Hades.

As the passage from Lucius Apuleius's *Golden Ass* quoted in a previous chapter shows, the goddess Isis had in the late Roman Empire absorbed all the ethnic goddesses of the Roman Empire. She thus become the quintessential Goddess par excellence, a tradition taken over by the Fellowship of Isis, a world-wide Goddess-worshipping organisation head-quartered in Ireland.

The Celtic names Brighd and Cerridwen are preferred by many British Pagan groups as being the indigenous goddesses before the Roman invasion, and thus the authentic goddesses of the land, and this practice has also been taken over by many North American Pagans.

As Paganism has spread to the Continent, many Dutch, German and Scandinavian Pagans have sought out their own native Pagan traditions among the Nordic goddesses Freyja, Frigga, Sif, Sigyn and Helle and their male consorts Odinn (Wotan), Thor and Loki.

As I have already mentioned in the previous chapter a Jewish Pagan movement has been created in the United States, to worship the Semitic goddess Asherah without denying JHVH, who has played such a key role in Jewish history.

Latin American Pagans in the *Voudun*, *Santeria*, *Candomble* and *Macumba* traditions have, of course, long worshipped the Yoruba female orishas Yemaya and Oshun, and the male orishas Ogun, Chango and Eleggua among others; either under their own names or those of Roman Catholic saints which their slave ancestors had adopted as cover in the days of Church persecution of their religion.

This raises the question whether these are just different ethnic names for the same world-wide or cosmic energies – and thus essentially interchangeable – or whether each ethnic pantheon has its own identity and links to the ethnic groups that worshipped it.

Are Goddesses and Gods Real?

Some contemporary Pagans see the goddesses and gods as poetic metaphors for processes beyond human understanding. Others, including myself, see them as real powers with whom it is possible to establish personal relationships.

Does *electricity* exist? You can't see it in its pure form, but you can see its effects. When turning a switch makes a light go on or starts up a motor, then you are driven to the conclusion that something is causing these things to happen, and you might as well call it 'electricity'.

The same goes for gods and goddesses. Postulated as immaterial, eternal and universal, nobody has ever seen one by the conscious light of day, but many of us have had occasion to observe their effects. Do they alter the personality of people on whom they are invoked? Do they answer prayers, or procure the results for which they have been invoked? The answer is 'Yes' more frequently than not.

Every god and every goddess that has ever been worshipped seriously in any part of the world can be invoked effectively by a receptive person, and has granted the wishes of most of the people who have prayed to or invoked them. This is true not just of the Pagan Great Mother and Horned God, but of the Egyptian Isis, Osiris, Nephtys, Nuit, Sekhmet and Ra; the Greek Aphrodite, Artemis, Zeus, Apollo, and all the other Olympians; the Babylonian Ishtar and Baal; the Yoruba Obatala, Eleggua, Yemaya, Ogun and Oshun; the Nordic Odin, Thor, Frigg, Freyr and Freya; yes, and also JHVH, Jesus Christ and Maria.

Who are these gods and goddesses who so readily answer the prayers of their devotees and can even possess them? Are some or all of them universal, or limited in space to a certain ethnic group or place? What are their relationships to each other, not just those belonging to the same mythological pantheon, but between pantheons?

According to quantum physics theory, everything in the Universe – including ourselves – is energy at different frequency levels. So the gods and goddesses too are 'energies', but less limited in time and space than we mortal animals. Our relationship to them might be compared to that of a drop of water to the river or ocean to which it belongs. When we invoke a god or goddess into ourselves or a fellow Pagan, we call on that divine energy to complement the person's energy, or even to take his/her body over completely for the duration of a ritual. When we pray to a god or goddess, we ask Him or Her to ripple the web of fate of the person for whom we are working.

But how did these divine energies arise in the first place, and what differentiates them one from another? Reading or listening to contemporary Pagans discussing these issues, there seem to be at least three theories about them which are not necessarily mutually exclusive.

81

1 The 'Thought-Form' or Spiritual Bank Account

Human minds can create new autonomous energy patterns called 'thought-forms', and we do it all the time. Many families create imaginary characters for their children's or their own amusement, who after a while take on a life of their own. Guru images, even national and regimental flags, are thought forms.

When a flag is recognised by the people of a nation or ethnic group and they start saluting it, they are banking some of their spiritual energy into that thought-form. So are the worshippers of any god or goddess or mythical or historical founder of their religion. Just as banks lend out to businesses or house buyers the money that has been deposited with them, so the energy banked in any thought-form – be it a flag or a god/dess – is available to any worshipper in need: be it a soldier whose resolve needs stiffening in the face of the enemy, or a spiritual healer or spell caster.

Whether or not that is all they are, all ethnic gods and goddesses have aspects of the thought-form about them, and give out the energy that their worshippers have deposited with them. So Thor, Perkunas and Chango are not completely inter-changeable when it comes to asking a thunder god for rain. If you invoke Thor, you will get a lot of Nordic and Germanic energy; Perkunas will give you Balt energy; while Chango will give you a lot of Yoruba and Latin American energy.

A number of people who started working with Odin in the last ten years found their political opinions suddenly shifting sharply to the Right, and became much more militarist and racially conscious, before wilfully moving back to their own centre. They had probably picked up some Nazi energy, as sections of the Nazi Party, notably Himmler, had adopted Odin as their ethnic god in the 1940s, and some neo-Nazi groups do so today. This does not mean that the original Viking Odin conforms to the Nazi stereotype – He is a far subtler, wiser and more imaginative character – but a great deal of Nazi energy had been banked with him.

For this reason, most Pagans distance themselves from Satanists, who worship or invoke Satan as the great rebel against the cruel genocidal god JHVH, and refuse to acknowledge them as members of the otherwise very broad Pagan community. For whatever Seth may have been in Egyptian mythology before the worshippers of Isis and Osiris demonised him, whom the Israelites then turned into their demon Shaitan, the Christian devil image Satan has for centuries been the repository of all the repressed sexual and sadistic imaginings of celibate Catholic priests and monks. Just look at the paintings of Hieronymus Bosch. That is the negative energy that people who invoke Satan today receive whatever their intent was. To get at the original Seth energy through this image is like searching for a pearl in a dung heap. Whether you find it or not, you come out of the experience covered in and smelling of shit!

What has saved most self-proclaimed Satanists and Luciferians from dire psychological consequences in recent years, is that they are mostly magically incompetent or just uninterested. Most of them are poseurs out to shock stuffy respectable society, be they teenagers rebelling against fundamentalist Christian parents, or a circus showman like Anton LaVey, founder and head of the Church of Satan. It is interesting that when Michael Aquino broke away from the Church of Satan to found a serious magical order (the Temple of Set), the deity he contacted told him to call Him Set not Satan, a name less likely to bring forth that negative mediaeval energy.

Occasionally, however, concentrating on negative anti-Christian rebellion and worshipping Christian demons can have tragic consequences for Satanists or Luciferians. In May 1995, the High Priestess and High Priest of an obsessively anti-Catholic French Luciferian group, who called themselves perversely *Wicca française*, as well as their chief disciple committed suicide.

Nor are all pre-Christian Pagan gods beneficent agricultural fertility figures. Some were tribal war gods as ruthless as the Jewish JHVH, sometimes more so. Most Pagans therefore study carefully the myths associated with each deity before we pray to or invoke them.

2 The Archetypal Image

According to Jung, certain god and goddess images remind us subconsciously of primal experiences that we share with all other human, indeed most living beings: Jung calls these *archetypal* images. They differ from thought-forms in that they were not created at a certain time, but go back to the dawn of human consciousness.

All human beings, like all mammals, grew as foetuses in a female mother's body. In most cases, the mother who bore them also looked after them until they were strong enough to fend for themselves. This makes the Mother Goddess image the most potent archetype in the human subconscious, and we recognise Her in all the ethnic mother goddesses of the various pantheons.

Even in fully functioning families, children become aware of their fathers only some time after birth, and develop a strong relationship with them only when they have become old enough to be trained by the father in manly skills (boys) or to discover gender polarity with him (girls). So the Father God archetype is not normally quite as powerful as the Mother Goddess, except in the three patriarchal monotheistic religions that have tried to suppress the Mother Goddess altogether.

There are many other archetypal images that reflect common facets of human experience of each other: the untouched Virgin, the seducing Vamp, the primal Lustful Male, the more Spiritual Lover, the Responsible Mate and Father, the Warrior, the Wise Old Wo/Man. Look at the twenty-two Major Arcana of the Tarot deck: they are all there! And most of them are also found in one form or another in most mythological pantheons.

3 The Gateway Image to a Cosmic Force

The boldest theory – held by most religious people – is that their god(s) and goddess(es) are anthropomorphic images to aid human understanding and relationship to cosmic forces, to which the god/dess images act as gateways. Thus Jews, Christians and Muslims see in JHVH not just a Semitic tribal god but the Creator of the Universe. Shaivite and Shaktiite Hindus see in Kali the primordial energy/matter of the Universe, who gave substance to the abstract forms that Her consort Shiva had conceived in His Creative Mind.

How can we distinguish between god/dess(es) that are gateways to cosmic forces, those that are archetypes of the human subconscious, and those that are no more than thought-forms created at a certain point in the history of a tribe? All three types can be invoked, and all three answer prayers and give help in magical spells.

Like most aspects of religious belief, the criteria are subjective. A first step is to study carefully the myths associated with a particular deity. If it is solely concerned with being the ancestor of and protecting a particular tribe, nation or culture, then it is probably a tribal thought-form, and will be difficult to invoke if you do not belong to that tribe, nation or culture.

If the deity addresses universal human experiences, like love, parenthood and death, and is magically accessible to anyone, then it is at the very least a human archetype. But if it is postulated to command the seas, the winds, the earth and its fertility, the sun, moon or the stars beyond, then it is a gateway image to an elemental or cosmic power.

Human belief tends to be self-fulfilling, and to give deities a great deal of their power. If, when invoking a god/dess to help you in a spell, you see in him or her no more than a created thought-form, then the only energy you will receive in return will be that which you and others have banked in that thought-form in the past.

If you conceive of your god/dess as a primal human archetypal image, then you will receive the collective human energy associated with that archetypical experience since the dawn of time.

But if you truly believe your god/dess is a gateway image to a cosmic power, then it is the power of the cosmos that will aid you in your spell, if you know how to handle it!

85

Duotheists versus Polytheists

A majority of English language Pagans – especially those belonging to or inspired by the Wiccan and Druid traditions – see 'all (ethnic) goddesses as expressions of the one Goddess, and all gods expressions of the one God.' They express this in Deena Mezger's chant popularised by Starhawk:

Isis, Astarte, Diana, Hecate, Demeter, Kali, Inanna

and its lesser known Horned God equivalent:

Pan, Herne, Baphomet, Cernunnos, Osiris.

This was clearly also the view of Lucius Apuleius, who saw Isis as incorporating not only all goddesses but all gods as well.

Nordic and Lithuanian Pagans, on the other hand, insist that their gods and goddesses have distinct energies and personalities and are not just different names for a single Goddess and God, though they would acknowledge them as 'daughters' and 'sons' of the original Goddess and God in their creation myths. They warn the untutored not to invoke an ethnic deity without previously studying the myths associated with Her or Him.

The more extreme even say that no one should worship or invoke an ethnic god/dess who does not descend from the ethnic group to which the deity concerned belonged. This is also the view of Native Americans, appalled at the plunder of their spiritual traditions by some New Age authors and workshop gurus.

I belong to the polytheist camp, for it seems to me that all goddess and god images have always been a blend of the cosmic force and the human thought-form. Invoke them and you get a mixture of cosmic energy, but also of the energy banked in the thought-form by previous worshippers.

Goddesses of the Land

In studying the old pre-Christian mythologies, we find a sharp distinction between the character of the various goddesses and gods.

The goddesses rule mostly over specific lands or cities, irrespective of which tribe happens to be living there at the time. Thus Pallas Athene was the patron goddess and protectress of the city of Athens and surrounding Attica; Vesta the protectress of Rome, Ishtar of Babylon. In so far as the functions of land goddesses are similar the world over, it is easier to see 'all goddesses as the expression of one Goddess' as Lucius Apuleius clearly did; but only up to a point.

Goddesses associated with a specific city or piece of land are clearly limited in space though not in time, and thus differ from the Goddess as a universal energy. They express the energy – atmosphere if you like – of a particular city or place. In this they are similar to the elemental spirits recognised by most esotericists, who are the soul and living energy of a specific stream, waterfall, wood, tree, garden, cloud or wind; the last two of course much more ephemeral than the former.

Some city goddesses later acquired universality. Isis, for instance, is believed by historians to have been originally a very human queen of the Egyptian city of Memphis. After Her death, She became that city's protector goddess. When Memphis conquered the whole of Egypt, She became the Egyptian Mother Goddess. After the Seleucid conquest of Egypt, She became the universal Goddess of the Seleucid empire, before becoming finally the supreme Goddess of a mystery cult in the Roman Empire.

Clearly, the Isis that appeared to Lucius in his dream in the 3rd century CE was a universal power quite different from the patroness of Memphis a couple of millennia earlier, let alone the original living queen of that city. The gradual universalisation of Her energy was partly the result of the beliefs and expectations of Her worshippers, thus altering Her character as a humanly created thought-form. But at some stage, this thought-form became the gateway image to the universal Goddess energy.

Something similar happened to the Yoruba orishas. They were originally guardian spirits of different West African towns and tribes. But when slaves from all parts of West Africa were chained together in the ships taking them as slaves to America, some orishas were invoked for protection and became universal forces. Yemaya, orisha of the Moon and the sea, became the most powerful of these because she had protected the life of those who made it across the Atlantic to the New World.

Tribal Gods

The male gods, on the other hand, fall into two groups:
- Neolithic fertility figures like Pan, Cernunnos and the Nordic Frey, also associated with the land like their companion goddesses; in Nordic mythology they are the Vanir;
- Indo-European tribal gods who moved with their tribes as they invaded Europe and India from the Caucasus or Central Asia: the Vedic, Olympian gods and the Nordic Aesir. Tribal gods are believed to have originated as real or mythical tribal ancestors, and their worship to be therefore a development from ancestor worship.

The battle between the Aesir and Vanir in Nordic mythology is a reflection of the battles between their human worshippers, as the Aesir-worshipping invaders met resistance from the land's original inhabitants.

The Indo-European invaders generally won, but sought to secure the allegiance of their new subjects by marrying their tribal gods to the goddesses of the land they had conquered, reflected on Earth by the forced marriage of the invaders' kings with the land's hereditary priestess-queens. Thus the Achaean Zeus married the Hellenic goddess Hera in Greek mythology, a marriage reflected on earth by the marriage of the Achaean king Atreus' two sons Agamemnon and Menelaos to the hereditary priestess queens Clytaemnestra of Argos and Helen of Sparta. In Northern Europe the Aesa Odin married the Vana Freyja; and in India the Vedic Vishnu married the Dravidian Lakshmi.

A North American syncretistic Pagan religion along the same lines would marry Celtic, Norse or Greek gods with Native American goddesses of the land if there are any.

Most Indo-European tribes had more than one god, and the different gods fulfilled different functions: war-god, thunder and weather god, magician, smith. After they married the goddesses of the lands their tribe had conquered their consort goddesses also became more universal but also functionally more specialised: Athene goddess of intellectual pursuits, Artemis of hunting, Aphrodite of love, Hera of stable (patriarchal) marriage.

It follows that many of the old Pagan gods have very sharply defined identities. Most Pagans therefore consider it wiser to invoke them only when one knows their exact attributes and wants to invoke precisely these. Although these attributes can change over time, the time-scales are considerable when matched against a single human life. Their energies are often closely associated with the temples and sacred sites at which they were worshipped in the past, and do not take kindly at all to other rites being performed at the same location, as the following story will show.

The Angry Thunder God

In October 1990 I joined a party of Californian Pagans from the Church of All Worlds (CAW) on a tour of the ancient sacred sites and Pagan temples of Peru. After a day in Lima, we flew to the former Inca capital of Cuzco, where we spent three days visiting some of the twenty Pagan temples in the hills around the city. These were carved out of natural rock formations during the Inca period or before, so that it was impossible for the Spanish conquerors to destroy them without dynamite, which they fortunately did not possess.

On the second day, we were taken by coach to visit the Thunder God's temple, accompanied by a local shaman – a mestizo with a university degree in anthropology, who had been impelled by the success of the Carlos Castaneda books in the West to study the old Quechua (the name of the indigenous inhabitants of Peru) religion with village shamans, and who was now teaching it to visiting American New Age parties. We were the first Western Pagan group he had met.

It was a clear sunny spring day, quite warm enough to sit in the temple listening to our guide explain the Quechua cosmology, its various gods, goddesses and power animals. After the lecture, he conducted a Quechua ceremony in honour of the Thunder God whose temple we were in.

When he had finished, a woman in our party suggested we show our respect by performing a CAW Pagan ritual. Hardly had we gathered in a circle around one of the stones than an angry storm-cloud suddenly appeared in the sky to our north racing towards the temple. When it was straight above us, it opened up and we were drenched in a downpour of rain. 'I feel like going on,' said the officiating priestess, and no one demurred. Within seconds, the rain turned to hail, and ice blocks the size of eggs started pelting us. At this point, wisdom prevailed. We broke off the circle and raced back to our bus. Within half a mile, we were back in dry sunny weather: the storm had been purely local.

'This has never happened before,' said our shaman guide diplomatically. 'It shows the Thunder God recognises you as very special people to be welcoming you in this way!' Some welcome! The god was clearly angry at this inconsiderate misuse of His temple for a ritual that He had not inspired.

Three days later we were in Machu Picchu, and our shaman guide took us on a two-hour mountain hike to a cave dedicated as temple to the Moon goddess. Once again, he explained the beliefs surrounding this deity and then conducted a ritual in Her honour at the cave's entrance in the open. As the ritual proceeded, we felt the site vibrate with Goddess energy, and a condor – one of the Quechua power animals – appeared overhead and circled over us: a true blessing that had 'also never happened before' according to our shaman guide. This time, no one spoiled the atmosphere by suggesting a Western Pagan ritual, and we trudged back happily on the two-hour trek back to our hotel.

Besides being a warning to Pagans and magicians of all hues not to misuse temples for other deities or purposes than the ones they are intended for, this story illustrates also my Pagan pantheistic mindset. I don't believe that anything in nature is an accident or a coincidence: nearly everything is willed by some energy for a purpose. The sudden downpour of rain over the temple of Thunder God while we were performing a Western Pagan ritual was not – in my mind – an accident, but an expression of the Thunder God's displeasure.

Nerthus Takes Umbrage

It isn't just thunder gods that object to alien rituals being performed at their sacred sites. The Goddess of the land also prefers to be invoked under Her local name by local or foreign visitors.

In August 1992 I was one of some 80 European Wiccans who held an eight-day camp in western Norway, on a mountain about halfway between Stavanger and Kristiansand. We arrived on a Friday and left on the Saturday eight days later. The day before our arrival our Norwegian hosts had asked the local goddess Nerthus for fine weather in a country notorious for its rains. Their prayers were rewarded with fine sunny weather, both on the Friday of our arrival and the following day.

The camp's programme had allocated each evening's ritual to a different participating national group. The opening ritual on the Saturday night was conducted by the British contingent invoking Greek gods and goddesses. Halfway through the ritual it started to rain, and went on raining all through the night and Sunday morning, but stopped around 3 in the afternoon. By the time of our evening ritual at 9 p.m., the sky had cleared to reveal a clear starlit night, so it was dry enough for an outdoor ritual.

This time it was the turn of some Lithuanian visitors to call

91

on their goddess and god. Their ritual was not interrupted, but in the middle of the night it started raining again, and went on raining all through the Monday morning until 3 p.m. when it stopped, and by 9 p.m. we again had a clear starlit night.

This weather pattern was repeated for three more days, as the Finns, the Germans and again the British conducted rituals. At last, on the Thursday evening, it was the turn of our Norwegian hosts: they had scheduled their Nerthus ritual last so as to give themselves extra time to rehearse it. This time it did not rain in the night and the Friday and Saturday of our departure were warm clear sunny days. If only we had invoked Nerthus every evening before invoking any of the other ethnic deities, we might have had sunny weather the whole week.

Ethnic Exclusiveness

If some deities at least like to be addressed only by their local names and have only accustomed rituals performed at their sacred sites, do they discriminate equally between the people who worship them? Would Nerthus have objected if a Norwegian-speaking English priestess had invoked Her? Or if She had been invoked in English or German?

Freya Aswynn, England's foremost Runemistress and volva, who has served Odin and studied the runes for over twelve years, used to think so. The Aesir, Vanir and runes were only for people with German or Scandinavian ancestry; other ethnic groups should worship their own gods and goddesses, and practise their own ethnic magical traditions. Native Americans feel the same way.

After Freya's book *Leaves of Yggdrasil* was published, first in England and then in America, she started receiving letters from other Odin worshippers around the world. To her astonishment, the letter with the deepest and most authentic understanding of Odin came from an Afro-Caribbean correspondent living in Haiti. 'Maybe he had a visiting German or Viking captain among his ancestors!' she said at first. More recently, however, she has discovered strong energy links between the Nordic Aesir and Vanir and the Yoruba orisha, even to the extent of Odin (when invoked on a person) showing a strong liking for cigars, which were unknown in Viking times, but which are an Eleggua favourite.

Similarly, Murry Hope, the writer on Egyptian ritual magic, says that Egyptian and Greek deities work well together, but not with the Jewish archangels of the Kabbalah.

Unexpected Guardian Deities

Two unexpected occurrences in my own life convinced me that ethnic deities – i.e. the energies that they represent – can act far away from their countries of origin.

Most Pagans believe that among the scores of deities of the world's mythologies one or two take a special interest in them as individuals, and are thus their 'guardian deities'. This means that their own personal energy frequency harmonises with that of the more universal guardian deity energy.

For the last 25 years I have prayed to or invoked various goddesses at crossroad trees in woods near my home most evenings. The name 'Goddess' appearing to me too impersonal, I experimented with various Greek and Egyptian goddess names in my invocations. 'Isis' produced the greatest resonance of them all, but it still wasn't the perfect fit.

In 1980, I spent a week in Abidjan, former capital of the Ivory Coast, as a lecturer in a seminar on computers. On the first day, I visited one of the native markets but found little to interest me. I had left the market and was returning to the hotel when an excited local man caught up with me and showed me a beautiful dark balsawood mask of a goddess figure with white cowrie shells and blue glass beads on her face, suggesting a connection with both the sea and the moon. He wanted £60 in local currency for it, which it was well worth, but I had only £15 in cash on me, and he finally let me have it for that amount.

I had not discussed religion with any of the market merchants, so my contact had no rational way of knowing that I

93

was a Goddess worshipper. But it was as if the mask itself had decided to enter my life and had informed its owner (or thief) of this. I took it home with me to England, hung it in my sitting room where it has exuded calm and serenity ever since.

Three years later I bought Migenes Gonzales-Wippler's book *Santeria*. It taught me that the name of the Yoruba sea and moon goddess is Yemaya. When I next prayed to the Goddess in the evening at my accustomed tree, I tried the name Yemaya. The resonance was immediate, much more powerful than any of the Greek or Egyptian names I had tried until then, stronger even than Isis.

In the meantime, I had embarked on a free-lance lecturing career on computers and needed an agent to organise bookings and collect fees for me. A small Swiss company named ANUBIT appealed to me because of the closeness of its name to the Egyptian god Anubis. So I employed them, and my fortunes improved immediately, turning the last fourteen years into the most successful and prosperous of my whole career. Nor is this the only way in which Anubis has helped me. I often mislay either my purse or my keys around the house. When I have looked five times at all the most obvious spots, I call on Anubis to help me and within a minute I normally find what I am looking for.

Two years ago, I was browsing in a Paris bookshop and found sets of astrological cards they were selling. In addition to the Western zodiac, they also sold cards on Egyptian and Chinese astrology. I had not heard of Egyptian astrology before, and learned that each two-week period in the year is under the protection of a different god or goddess, who becomes the guardian deity of those born during that period. My birthday is on 5 July, so I looked up the deity protecting the first half of July: it is the god Anubis.

Ethnically, I am half Austrian on my father's side, quarter Scottish and quarter Jewish on my mother's side. If the ethnic exclusivists were correct, therefore, I should have a German guardian god, and a Celtic or Semitic guardian goddess. Yet my guardian goddess is Yoruban, and my guardian god Egyptian.

A Universal Black Goddess?

It is also possible that Yemaya's mask has a wider significance than just to tell me who my personal guardian Goddess is. During the last millennium and a half, when the Church drove the old Celtic, Norse, Greek and Egyptian deities underground and starved them of human worship, the Yoruban orishas continued to be worshipped openly and actively. The infamous slave trade took them to the Caribbean and both Americas, and Yemaya became the most powerful of them all, because She protected the slaves on the long sea journey.

Now worshipped by millions of people in Latin America and among the Latinos in the United States, Yemaya may have become the new Isis: the Goddess who subsumes all other goddesses within Herself. To re-establish an equilibrium between our overdeveloped rational and technological minds, and our starved emotions and intuitions, perhaps we Western people need to re-establish not just the worship of a Goddess, but of a Black Goddess from the much abused continent whose exploited people know more than any others what strength there is in sensuality, joy and laughter!

Significantly enough, there is among Italian feminists a cult of Black Virgins, whose altars in old country churches are believed to exude much more power and Goddess energy than the pale-complexioned Virgins of ordinary churches.

8

Community Festivals and Worship

Every religion has its social as well as its metaphysical side: its purpose is to link (Latin = *religere*) not just individual worshippers to their god(s) and/or goddess(es), but also to each other. Contemporary Western Paganism is no different; our social worship comprises:

1. seasonal festivals,
2. seasonal or annual gatherings,
3. monthly or more frequent circles.

Seasonal Festivals

Festivals play a very important part in every religion: they are usually centred around a ritual drama that re-enacts one or more of the religion's main beliefs or myths, and thereby strengthens its hold on participants' beliefs. In the three monotheistic historical religions, all festivals celebrate some historical event:

– the Israelites leaving Egypt (Passover)
– the birth of Jesus (Christmas)
– Jesus' crucifixion (Good Friday) and Resurrection (Easter),
– Mohammed fleeing Mecca for Medina.

96

Their celebration reinforces the participants' belief in the importance of linear history and of the evolution of their religious beliefs.

In sharp contrast, Pagan festivals are not concerned with historical events but with the ever-recurring cyclicity of life. The Druid orders tend to celebrate the two solstices and two equinoxes with colourful ceremonies by day at some historical sacred site: Tower Hill or Parliament Hill in London, Stonehenge, Avebury, and equivalent sites in other countries.

Wiccan-inspired festivals celebrate mainly the four cross-quarter days: Imbolc or Candlemas on February Eve (31 January), Beltaine on May Eve (30 April), Lughnasad or Lammas on August Eve (31 July), and Samhain or Halloween on November Eve (31 October), but sometimes celebrate the solstices and equinoxes as well. They take place in the evening and normally occur on the Saturday night before or just after the due date, so that people can prepare for them free of work-related stress, as mental and psychic states are important in Pagan rituals.

Many Pagans believe that festivals are most effective in attuning the participants to natural cycles if celebrated out of doors, on a 'power spot' where religious festivals were celebrated in the pre-Christian Pagan past: usually a hill or mountain top with a good view of the surrounding countryside. In practice, this is not always possible, especially for Pagans living in big metropolises like London. When it isn't, the organising Pagan group usually hire a hall, and charge a small entrance fee to the event to defray the rental expense.

The form of these festivals varies between groups. Some have set forms for each festival that they re-enact every year, others rewrite it afresh on each occasion. But in practice, the form is very similar. As people arrive, they are offered wine and other refreshments, and then gather in small groups of friends to chat. When the formal part of the meeting begins, all participants gather in a large circle and hold hands, while the officers of the ceremony invoke the guardians of the four quarters (E, S, W and N) to watch over the proceedings: this has the effect of 'centre-ing' all the participants in the place where they find themselves, and to confine their attention to what is going on inside the circle.

This done, the group who have organised the festival usually perform a short ritual drama of the mythical events that are supposed to take place on the divine plane at this time of the year. When the ritual drama is over, participants are invited to join in some traditional Pagan songs. A cup of wine or mead and some bread or cakes are then consecrated and passed around. The circle is then formally closed, and the meeting becomes a typical party with much feasting, drinking and dancing.

Each festival celebrates an event in the cycle of the seasons. Some groups dramatise this as a rite of passage for the God of the solar and vegetation year, who represents each year's unique identity in relationship to the eternal and immortal three-fold Goddess.

At **Yule** (winter solstice) the new solar year is born to the Mother Goddess. While Pagan communities as a whole celebrate this event with a dance and social, within Pagan families the focus is on children and presents to them, as indeed it is in Christian families at Christmas, that most Pagan of Christian festivals. When an adult dresses up as Father Christmas, it is because we see him as a very Pagan figure: Old Father Time bringing the newborn year the gifts of the experience and wisdom of previous generations.

At **Imbolc** or **Candlemas**, the new solar year makes itself known by now noticeably longer days. It is also a time when lambs are born to the sheep in the fields. So the time has come to celebrate the return of the light with candles.

At the **Spring Equinox,** day and night are equal. **Easter,** on the first Sunday after the first full moon after the Spring Equinox, is named after the goddess Ostara, and marks the beginning of spring in southern European countries. The eggs that are hidden in the garden and the hares or bunny rabbits are clear fertility symbols.

Beltaine is the alternative Spring festival for England, Central Europe and equivalent latitudes elsewhere, and one of the two most important festivals in the Wiccan calendar. Our

98

farming ancestors celebrated this by making love in the fields to ensure the fertility of the crops, in the spirit of this old rhyme:

Hooray, hooray for the first of May,
Outdoor loving starts today!

Few contemporary Pagans have private gardens sufficiently secluded to be able to do this, though some intrepid groups go to public woodlands sufficiently far from the nearest town or village to be reasonably certain that they will not be disturbed. It would be interesting to do this around some Pagan farmer's field and then compare the subsequent richness of its crop with that of neighbouring fields which had not been so blessed.

Midsummer (solstice) is the high point of the solar year, who is then in his prime. It is also the fertility festival in Scandinavia when young people dance around bonfires on hilltops all night and many couples disappear into the bushes. In other countries it is often a favourite time for Pagan couples to be 'handfasted', the marriage we undertake when we have lived together for some time and know each other well enough to be confident of being able to live together in affection and amity to raise a family and beyond.

Lammas (August Eve) and the **Autumn Equinox** are both harvest festivals: for wheat and other cereals at the end of July; grapes and other fruit in September. In England, some groups celebrate the traditional sacrifice of John Barleycorn, the spirit of the crops, who lays down his life that the community may be fed.

At the Equinox, day and night are once again equal. Some Wiccan groups re-enact the fight between the Oak King and the Holly King, while others dramatise the Earth Goddess' return into the underworld, Her task for the year accomplished. She leaves the God of the vegetation year alone and widowed above. Without Her nourishing presence, He like the trees and plants, slowly dries up until He finally dies at:

Samhain or **Halloween** (November Eve), the Wiccan festival of the dead, and the other most important festival of the year. We gather the dead branches of trees fallen to the ground and build great bonfires, in whose ashes we bake potatoes and cook chestnuts or sausages while drinking hot punch, beer or mead. In the shadows of the flickering flames, the spirits of our dear departed join us.

By then, there are only a little over seven weeks to go before the next **Yule**, when the next solar year will be born, and the ghost of the dead year will join Old Father Time in wishing the newborn infant well and bringing him the gifts of the wisdom of past generations.

Just as the sun always returns after the winter solstice, and each winter is followed by a fresh spring, so the participants at these festivals slowly absorb the subliminal message that their own death, when it finally comes, will not be the end. After a period of restful oblivion in the underworld, they too will return as infants to play a fresh role on the scene of life.

The climate's influence

Since the purpose of Pagan seasonal festivals is to attune us more to the natural cycles of life, I feel we could with advantage listen more to the rhythms of Nature to determine the dates of our festivals than to the Gregorian solar calendar: not just as between climatic zones, but from year to year. Though as urban Pagans most of us don't have the opportunity of observing the exact time when ewes begin to lamb in the spring, or when the cereal crops are ripe for cutting, we might still take the blossoming of certain flowers and trees as the signal for our festivities.

In the Hampstead Garden Suburb in North London in which I used to live, spring was always signalled to me by the blossoming of the cherry trees that line the main residential streets. This could vary from year to year between mid-April and mid-May, though it mostly happens at the beginning of May. But in 1990, a freak heat wave of 70°F (21°C) during the last week of February caused the cherry trees to bloom at that time: that is when we should have celebrated Beltaine in that year.

All the same, our present festival dates map fairly well on to the English, Dutch and German climates. Not so, however, when we cross the Atlantic to North America or the Indian Ocean to Australia: yet many American and Australian Pagan groups stick to the festival dates laid down in England, without observing the cycles of their nature around them.

Others, however, have adapted. The most thoughtful is a group in Los Angeles, who have observed that the desert vegetation around them dies and goes brown in the searing heat of summer, only to revive when the rains come in the autumn. So they celebrate the festival of Death at midsummer, and the festival of the rebirth of life at Halloween.

Gatherings

Whereas the four to eight seasonal festivals are usually celebrated during one afternoon, evening or perhaps – at Beltaine or Halloween – one night, gatherings are camps that last longer: a long weekend of three days and nights, or a whole week. Some are public and advertised in Pagan publications, while others are private to a certain Pagan ritual tradition and by invitation only. A group of Pagans will hire a camp site for the period, with accommodation in camping huts or in tents, with communal cooking and meals.

During the gathering, the participating Pagans seclude themselves as much as possible from the outside world. Each day begins and ends with a religious ritual in which all participate. In between, there are a large number of lectures and discussion groups on Pagan topics, as well as workshops on Pagan skills like making broomsticks and magical tools, Tarot card reading, astrology, folk dancing, dowsing and meditation, running in parallel. Each is organised by a different participant who has volunteered for the purpose. If there are any sacred Pagan sites in the vicinity – such as a Neolithic stone circle – an excursion will normally be organised to visit it halfway through the gathering.

101

Naturally, these gatherings occur mostly during the peak vacation period, between midsummer and the autumn equinox, though some American gatherings take place as early as Easter or May. All are an opportunity for Pagans from different parts of America or different European countries to meet each other, whereas the public festivals draw their participants mostly from the same urban area. Gatherings thus play a vital role in pulling different Pagan traditions together, and help us experience that we are all part of a world-wide movement.

Circles

Between seasonal festivals, some Pagans gather weekly, bi-monthly or monthly in small circles of close friends, sharing a common Pagan tradition: Wiccan covens, Druid groves, Fellowship of Isis 'Iseums', Church of All Worlds nests. There are also some *ad hoc* training groups in meditation, visualisation and ritual techniques. Some, like the Wiccan covens about which I shall write in the last part of this book, are part of an esoteric magical tradition that requires prior initiation; others are more informal. But they all have three features in common:

(1) participants sit and stand in circles during the proceedings,
(2) they are small, averaging six to eight members,
(3) they are private and only admit new members whom existing members like and trust, whatever their beliefs, experience and qualifications may be.

The circle is the main form of Pagan activities: at seasonal festivals as well as gatherings, people typically form circles for any kind of group ritual or discussion. It symbolises both the Goddess' womb and Eternity, since it is the only geometric form without beginning and without end. But on a practical level, it makes all the participants equal and allows two-way communication. Any member of a circle can speak and be heard equally well by all the circle's other members.

This can only happen, however, if the circle is kept small, determined by the number of people who can sit or stand comfortably in a circle in a typical private living room. This allows all the members to know each other very well, and it gives even the shyest among them the confidence to express their point of view. It also allows the group to arrive at an intuitive consensus on what its activities of the evening or the next few meetings will be, without formal motions and votes.

As soon as the size of a group grows above thirteen (the formal limit to Wiccan covens, though it is not always strictly adhered to), discussions begin to be dominated by the more exhibitionistic members, usually men. This can only be prevented by formalising discussions, with a chairperson calling on individual members to speak, and with decisions taken by formal vote afterwards, which inhibits spontaneity and creates distances between members.

Confidence on the part of even the shyest to open up their hearts and confide what may be troubling them, or on the contrary to share a recent joy, is also possible only in a small group, and one in which all members trust, like and are fond of each other. It only takes a clash between two incompatible personalities to ruin the atmosphere of a small group. This is why the subjective criteria of admission to the group are so vital, however much pain and resentment they may cause people with personality problems who find it difficult to be admitted to such groups.

Sharing of joys and problems is the main activity of all such groups. Those that are part of a magical tradition may follow this with a magical or spellcasting ritual, to help members or known friends with their problems. When no one has a problem that needs help, the group may use its magical energy to heal the Earth and/or to strengthen peace, understanding and tolerance in the general collective unconscious.

The small group is not just a Pagan feature; it seems to be the paradigm for the coming age's collective worship, even among Christians. While formal church congregations are falling year by year, there is said to be a boom in 'house churches': groups

103

of like-minded friends meeting in a private house for collective worship in which all participate. This is happening not just among those Protestant traditions that have always affirmed the priesthood of all believers like Quakers, Baptists and Congregationalists, but even among many Roman Catholics, who find the Mass more meaningful in a private house than in a large dark gloomy church.

A Voluntary Part-time Priesthood

Obviously, the driving force behind the formation of each new Pagan circle is usually a more experienced person, trained in magic, meditation, ritual and/or group therapy and dynamics, and the circle will meet in her/his home. (S)he thus plays the role of parish minister or priest(ess) to the circle's other members.

But with 'parish' membership limited usually to four to twelve other members, mostly of quite modest means, it is obvious that this must be a voluntary unpaid role, and therefore part-time, since the host priest(ess) will also have to earn her/his living or run a household. The circle's other members will usually contribute towards the evening's refreshments, ritual supplies and photocopying expenses.

A luxury?

This chagrins a small number of prominent Pagans, mostly in America, who would like to devote themselves full-time to publicising and teaching Paganism, and find the time they have to spend earning their living as management consultants, computer programmers, publishers or secretaries a waste of their talents. Since small groups cannot support a paid priest or minister, they argue that the small group is a luxury that the Pagan movement can no longer afford as it grows in numbers and is on the threshold of becoming a mass movement. Time, they say, to adopt the parish-congregation form of worship of other mass religions like Christianity and Judaism.

This is like saying that family houses are all very well in

104

sparsely populated Alpine valleys, but that in densely populated metropolises people have to live in communal dormitories. Just as even in the biggest metropolises all residential areas have rows upon rows of single family houses, or at least apartments, there is no reason why there should not be two or three small Pagan groups on every block should Paganism ever become a majority religion.

A part-time voluntary priesthood is thus the price that Pagans – and, it seems, many other religious traditions – have to pay to keep their basic groups small, equal and interactive. And the need to earn their living in the outside world helps to keep the part-time priest(ess)'s feet on the ground and in touch with everyday reality. The Pagan historian Prudence Jones points out that the priesthoods in Ancient Greece and Rome were also voluntary and unpaid.

Some Pagans with a calling to be full-time priest(esse)s have resolved their dilemma by leaving well-paid managerial or consultancy jobs to train in the near-priestly vocation as healer: psychotherapist, acupuncturist, reflexologist, or one of the many alternative forms of holistic healing available today.

Full-time Paid Regional Organisers

If no Pagan circle can afford to pay a full-time priest(ess), the time is approaching when all the Pagans of a large metropolitan area like Greater London or Greater New York may be able to afford one or more full-time organisers. But these will be largely public relations and administrative roles: lobbying public authorities for equal recognition of Paganism as a religion, writing to newspapers to correct misinformation, running information courses, organising public festivals, publishing journals, all being activities that are still done by volunteers at the moment. There will be no 'power over' others in such a full-time paid role, nothing to compare to the power of a Roman Catholic, Anglican or Episcopalian bishop.

9

Pagan Ethics

Eight words the Wiccan Rede fulfil:
An' it harm none, do what you will.

Although Wicca is only one of many contemporary Pagan
traditions, most Pagans would subscribe to the same ethic.
This strikes many Jews and Christians as anarchic antinomian-
ism, and the more bigoted among them suspect us of all sorts
of antisocial activities, from rampant promiscuity to child
sexual abuse.

Fallen versus Divine Humanity

Christian alarm at Pagan ethics expresses their fundamentally
different view of human nature from our own. Christians view
human nature as essentially *fallen* and *sinful*: human beings
cannot, therefore, be trusted to behave ethically toward each
other if they are not fenced in by explicit divine prohibitions,
and granted extra spiritual help by a Saviour who took all their
sins and their due punishment upon Himself. Although the
biblical Fall occurred when Adam and Even disobeyed one of
God's prohibitions, in practice the Christian churches appear
to regard mainly our emotional and instinctual drives as sinful,
because they prevent us from behaving as wholly rational
beings.

Pagans, on the other hand, regard all aspects of human nature – the spiritual and the physical, the rational and the emotional – as belonging to the divine Life-Force incarnate in each one of us. If we keep them in harmonious balance, we will survive best not only as individuals but as members of human collectivities.

'An it harm none...'

In practice, the proviso 'An it harm none' is far more demanding than the Ten Commandments. For the 'none' whom we should not harm includes not just all other human beings, but all living things and the planet's whole ecology.

This leads many Pagans into vegetarianism or even veganism, since they feel that one cannot eat any animal's meat or even its eggs or milk without harming it or its calf. But plants are also living beings with feelings, and since our metabolism demands that we eat either animal or vegetable produce – ideally a balanced combination of both – it seems that we cannot survive without 'harming' some living beings or others.

Other Pagans regard this as too extreme an interpretation. Paganism means living in harmony with Nature, and the food chain is part of Nature. But all Pagans would agree that all plants and animals should be allowed to live as normal a life as possible up to the point of their harvesting or slaughter, which should be as painless as possible. We all view intensive factory farming with horror, with its veal crates, chicken batteries and poisoning of the soil through overdoses of fertilisers and insecticides. Most of us buy only free range eggs and chickens and organic vegetables when these are available in our neighbourhood, even though they cost double the normal produce. We cannot unfortunately control what is served to us in restaurants.

Many of us sympathise with the Native American principle that one should only eat the meat of an animal that one has killed oneself, in a religious ceremony commending its soul to the guardian spirit of its species, or whose like one has had the

107

experience of killing at least once in the past, though I admit it is a principle I have not myself yet fulfilled.

Killing an animal in a dignified manner that recognises it as being endowed with spirit is incidentally the whole purpose of religious 'blood sacrifices' in the Bengali temples of Kali, and in West African religions and their Latin American derivatives Voudun, Santeria, Macumba and Candomble. The double thinking of people who throw up their hands in horror at such 'barbarous' religious practices, and who then with good conscience sit down to eat veal from a crate or a battery chicken, never ceases to amaze me.

The same principles inform our attitudes towards blood sports. Wild animals live more natural lives than domesticated cows or chickens. Therefore meeting one's body's protein requirements by eating game shot during a hunt is preferable to eating domesticated beef or chickens; as long as the hunt is confined to those animals one will consume afterwards and which do not belong to a protected species in danger of extinction. This is a different story altogether from those hunters who compete on who can shoot most partridges, or who spend an afternoon on horseback in red costume hunting down some unfortunate fox which, if they succeed in cornering it, they will then throw to their dogs to be torn to pieces. It will surprise no one that some Pagans also belong to hunt saboteur groups.

Many Pagans are also prominent ecological activists. In North America, some are members of Earth First, which uses direct action to oppose the vandalous clear cutting of California's millennia-old redwood trees by commercial timber companies inspired by financial greed. In England, two of the groups who campaigned on the spot against the desecration of Twyford Down and the M11 Extension – Dragon and the Dongas tribe – count themselves as Pagans. Those without the time for direct action will still do what we can by writing letters to newspapers and our MPs.

If Pagans have such sensitive consciences in our dealings with animals, plants and areas of outstanding beauty, it follows that most of us have no problems in dealing sensitively

108

and ethically with our fellow human beings. We regard all of them, regardless of race, creed, gender or sexual preference as fellow incarnations of the divine Life-Force, and our freedom of action ends at the boundary where theirs begins.

Living a Healthy Life

Somewhat surprisingly not all Pagans regard as yet their own bodies as part of the 'none' that should not be harmed. Pagans are as likely to be addicted cigarette smokers or alcoholics as other members of the class from which we come: less among the professional classes, more among industrial workers; less in North America, more in Europe. In North America, where pressure against smoking in public is stronger than in Europe and is turning compulsive overeating into an alternative relief from tension, Pagans are as likely as other members of the public to be 'horizontally challenged'.

Work Ethics

Pagans differ also in their attitudes to work in contemporary industrial society. Some regard any work for an industrial or commercial company, be it as employee or outside contractor, as conniving at the rape of the planet. The only jobs they would regard as clean are teaching, nursing, psychotherapy, holistic healing, growing or selling organic vegetables or running a Pagan book shop. Some live in intentional communities that try to be as self-sufficient as possible.

'Techno-Pagans' like myself regard that as too extreme a position. Those of us who work in the newer electronic, telecommunications and computer industries know these to be much less polluting than the older heavy industries dating from the 19th century. The Information Highway being slowly built in the advanced countries holds the promise of 'telecommuting' to work, thus eliminating the waste of human and fossil fuel energy involved in the daily journeys to and from the office, and in much business travel. The answer for us lies in contributing to the best of our abilities to hastening these developments and planning the fastest and smoothest possible transition from the industrial to the post-industrial society.

Nonetheless, Techno, as much as other Pagans, are generally allergic to working in large hierarchical companies. We much prefer to be self-employed or to run small companies of not more than 30 people composed largely of our friends. It is perhaps because the opportunities to do so are much greater in the computer industry that so many Pagans work in this field.

Do What You Will!

If the imperative 'An it harm none' is going to circumscribe so severely not only our dealings with fellow human beings but what we eat, drink and smoke, and where and how we work, what does the freedom to do what we will amount to in practice?

It certainly does not mean following every whim of the moment, nor ruining our health with over-indulgence! It means listening very carefully to our inner voices telling us what our own personal vocations are, and then pursuing these uncompromisingly, if necessary against the opposition of our parents or in the face of fashion or public opinion.

Those of us, for instance, who became Pagans and Goddess-worshippers 30 or 40 years ago, did so at a time when this was an insignificant minority religion, and our practice – if known – brought ridicule and derision on us at best, at worst it could cost us our careers. We did so because we had received the Goddess' call in one way or another, and we thus had to follow Her and thereby our own true will.

In a less dramatic way, those who become teachers, nurses, doctors or healers, often at considerable financial sacrifice, when they could have entered a much better paid position in a family firm or in the City, are 'doing what they will.'

Sexual Ethics

The injunction 'An it harm none' keeps all the Pagans I know from cheating, stealing, beating up or killing other people. Our practical ethics are 90 per cent the same as those of Jews, Christians and Muslims. The only area where our principles differ sharply from theirs is in sexual ethics.

To Pagans, sexual intimacy before marriage is neither sinful nor immoral, as long as it causes no physical or emotional harm to one's partner. On the contrary, we regard shared sexual passion under most circumstances as a sacrament which, far from harming our souls, can be a gateway to self-transcendence and union with the divine as I found in Mary's arms forty years ago. We believe in free love for both sexes, which includes the freedom *not* to love someone who loves or desires us, as well as to stay monogamously faithful to our current partner if that is what we have both agreed.

At the same time, we respect Nature and the nature of the sexual drive in human beings, which is intimately bound up with the emotions. Most Pagans who sleep together do so because they love or at least are very fond of each other. But we also acknowledge the validity of (apparently) pure physical lust for another person, and therefore of the one-night stand after an arousing dance or festival, as long as it is honest in its intent and accepts 'No' for an answer from a would-be partner who does not feel the same desire.

I wrote 'apparently' before pure physical lust, because in my experience a spontaneous desire for an unknown person one has just met is rarely if ever caused just by her or his vital statistics. One is usually picking up the other person's emotional vibrations unconsciously and finding these unusually compatible with one's own. If they truly are, the passion will usually be mutual, and the intended one-night stand may be the beginning of a long and successful relationship.

Most Pagans of both sexes practise serial monogamy in our late teens, twenties and early thirties in our search for the partner with whom we can be certain of being able to live amicably and happily for the rest of our lives. In this we are no

111

different from most of our Western contemporaries. Whether a couple decide to stay sexually monogamous during their relationship, or to give each other the freedom of having other intimate friendships simultaneously, is entirely up to them. Stable polyamorous relationships are still rare among European Pagans, though becoming more common in California.

What most Pagans despise is any form of deception: the man (it usually is a man) who pretends to love a woman he does not care for, just so she will satisfy his sexual needs; or the Lothario who has two or three intimate affairs in parallel but lets each partner believe that she is the only one.

Giving Children a Stable home

Few Pagans on either side of the Atlantic have children early. We are usually sufficiently well educated to know all about contraception, and many Pagans choose not to have any children at all. This may seem a surprising choice for the followers of a Nature religion, but it indicates our sensitivity to the problems caused by overpopulation. Those who have children tend to have them fairly late, when we are already in our thirties, being reasonably confident that we have found the partner with whom we can spend the rest of our lives in harmony.

Our educational practice is no different from our contemporaries'. We treat our children not just with love but as persons from the earliest age, who are entitled to explanations for the rules we have to lay down. But our pantheist convictions make this easier, since we regard our children too as incarnations of the divine, from whom we may have as much to learn as they from us.

Respecting the Age of Consent

Since we feel no guilt about premarital or even extra-marital sex (when it is with the consent of our partners), why has no Pagan yet been found guilty of sexual intimacy with an under-age child, unlike so many Roman Catholic and Anglican priests?

Because we only enjoy sexual intimacy with our equals in

emotional power, which children under the age of 16 generally are not. Sexual intimacy forced on prepubertal children by an adult is a traumatic violation, and even pubescent adolescents find it difficult to say 'No' to an older person. Besides, much sexual abuse of children or adolescents is not premeditated, but a spontaneous surrender to frustrated and repressed sexual drives that have become uncontrollable. Pagans are much less likely to suffer such frustrations, because we don't repress our sexual drives, but enjoy them without guilt with our equals.

The Merits of Self-love

'I do the things I would not do, and I do not do the things I should do!' wrote the apostle Paul nearly two thousand years ago, and his confession has been echoed by countless Christians ever since: it is the essence of the Christian sense of *sin*. What keeps Pagans from transgressing our own partly looser, but also partly more demanding, ethical principles?

Our self-confidence and self-love. We hold no impossible ideals of chastity and sexual continence in adulthood, and so have fewer reasons to be disgusted with ourselves. If we received plenty of love from our parents when we grew up, and from our partners and friends in adulthood, we find it easy to love ourselves, and, therefore, *to love our neighbours as we love ourselves*.

If some Christians find this so much more difficult, it is because they find it impossible to live up to their unnecessarily Puritanical code of conduct, and are thus filled with a sense of personal unworthiness, which they then project on others, especially those with different religious convictions than their own. They may then end up *hating* their neighbours as they *hate* themselves!

The Law of Return

Those of us who might be tempted nonetheless to behave in an unethical manner are mostly deterred by the Law of Return, also often called by the Sanskrit word *karma*. This means

113

simply that we reap as we sow, and that whatever we do comes back to us in the end. It is not some law written down in some holy book and administered by an angel or saint in the sky; it is a simple law of cause and effect which anyone can observe.

The person who is habitually kind, generous and tolerant will usually find it easy to make plenty of friends, who are the greatest reward that life can give us. The rude, mean and intolerant, on the other hand, will soon lose what friends they had and find themselves lonely and unloved.

If you want to pursue a career of theft and robbery, you will soon find yourself in the company of other thieves and robbers, some of whom will have no compunction of cheating and robbing you. If you try and get rich by gambling in casinos or the Stock Exchange, you will end up losing more money than you ever made. If you habitually deceive your partner, (s)he will grow to distrust and then despise you, and may leave you just when you need him or her most. If you neglect your children in their infancy, they will never visit you in your old age.

Some people seem to get away with an awful lot in this life without incurring retribution. Pagans believe them to be the unlucky ones, for the Law of Return will catch up with them in the next life or the one after that, when they will not remember their misdeeds in this life and wonder why it is their lot to be lonely and friendless. This does not mean that we turn our backs on the unfortunate among us, or that we say they brought it on themselves in a previous life. We don't interpret the Law of Return for others, just take it as a warning for ourselves. Mostly, however, we behave ethically and lovingly not out of fear of the Law of Return, but because it comes naturally to us.

The Problem of Evil

If ethical behaviour is so easy, why is there so much evil – exploitation, misery, drunkenness, degradation, violence – in the world? A problem that has been exercising theologians of all religions for centuries.

Let us be quite clear that 99 per cent of all the evil in the world is caused not by deviant individuals but by the abuse of state power, especially in wars. More women were probably raped by the Bosnian Serb forces in a few months than were raped by frustrated individuals in the whole of Europe during the previous twenty years. The personal possessions stolen by burglars are a small fraction of the possessions destroyed during the bombing of a city.

Why do so many governments behave in such a predatory, oppressive and destructive manner? Because of their lust for power over their citizens, and those of any territory that their state may once have controlled. This is a pathological reaction by people who lacked love and recognition from their parents in their childhood, and can now only respect themselves if they exercise power over and inspire fear in others.

This is the fruit of centuries of patriarchal monotheism, that suppressed all worship of the divine feminine with its values of love, sensuality and enjoyment of life, and supercharged the drives for material acquisitiveness and the exercise of power. The same psychological factors are leading many on the political Right to call for the dismantling of welfare state provisions to relieve poverty, sometimes paradoxically in the name of 'family values'.

The Pagan solution to the problem of evil is to re-establish the worship of the Earth Mother Goddess and Her daughter/ aspect: the Goddess of Love and Sensuality. The more that people feel free to love and be loved without guilt, the fewer will be driven to acquire more goods than they need to live comfortably, which will lead to a fairer distribution of the Earth's resources. The fairer resource distribution is, the fewer will be tempted to redress the balance by criminal activities.

The greater the proportion of people who have been loved and love themselves, the fewer the number of psychopaths driven to seek more power over others, to climb to the top in politics and, having got there, to use state power to unleash predatory and destructive wars.

10

Pagans and Other Religions

Just as there are no required Pagan beliefs, other than the reverence for Nature as expression of the divine whereby we define ourselves, there are no forbidden ones. We are free to combine membership of a Pagan circle with any other religious practice we find congenial: there are no Pagan authorities that could forbid this. Most Pagans are naturally curious and religiously syncretistic, and tend – in the words of one prominent Pagan – to 'appropriate any myth or idea that doesn't run too fast to get away!'

However, as I have already observed above, religions are not gratuitous aesthetic choices, but mental maps of our spiritual environment and of the cosmos, which in turn produce a certain type of behaviour. People who practise two or more religions in parallel should, therefore, ask themselves very seriously whether their respective maps and ethics are compatible with each other. If they are not, practising them in parallel will only produce spiritual confusion, and the benefit of both religions will be lost.

However, if our religious convictions – immanence of the divine in all human beings as well as plants and animals, equal divinity of women and men – truly express our age's needs and those of the next millennium, we would expect to see them emerge in other religious traditions as well: gods and goddesses have never respected confessional boundaries.

Let us therefore look at the main contemporary religious and philosophical movements, and consider to what extent these are compatible with contemporary Western Paganism, or are beginning to incorporate our values. The judgements are my own.

Feminism

Feminism is a political rather than religious movement, but it is the one with which contemporary Western Paganism has the greatest affinity. We both see the mindless exploitation and waste of the Earth's natural resources, the growing pollution, the dangerous tinkering with destructive thermonuclear and genetic engineering technologies, and aggressive militaristic foreign policies as the product of patriarchy, and see the solution in the re-establishment of a balance between masculine and feminine energies and values.

In pursuit of this goal, the religious wing of the Feminist movement adopted the Goddess as a 'symbol of self-empowerment for women' in the 1970s and has become one of the recognised traditions within the Pagan movement. While a few Feminists with a Christian background tried to take over Jehovah and put Him into skirts, most religious Feminists have the same immanent and cyclical concept of the Goddess as Earth Mother and Life-Force as Pagans. Starhawk, whose book *The Spiral Dance* was the first intellectually respectable description of modern Paganism and witchcraft, weaves her feminism, paganism and support for ecological causes into a seamless web of convictions.

Except in the minds of a few separatist extremists on whom the media seem to focus, there is no mutual incompatibility between membership of an all-women consciousness-raising group, and of a mixed gender Pagan group. Many women come from oppressive patriarchal families, in which mother and daughters had to keep silent when the father was speaking: they are then often inhibited from expressing themselves in the presence of men. Membership of an all-women's group helps them to gain self-confidence in the value of their own feelings and the right to express them.

After years in all-women groups, many such women have gained enough self-confidence to feel they can take on men on equal terms, and then join a mixed gender Pagan group. That is when they discover the Horned God as the Goddess' mate. Others continue in all-women groups, but this need not necessarily be an expression of gender separatism and hostility to men. In many tribal societies women also practise women's magic alone with other women while deeply committed to their husbands, sons and male friends.

There are nonetheless differences of emphasis. Pagans seek to re-establish harmony between humanity and Nature, and therefore accept all aspects of Nature, though not necessarily their interpretation by contemporary science. Some branches of Feminism, on the other hand, contain a streak of normativeness that can become at times authoritarian and oppressive.

Gender Differences Some Feminists assert as a dogma that the only natural differences between men and women are in the physical construction of their genital areas: all the traditional behavioural differences are the product of patriarchal culture and upbringing, designed to keep men dominant and women submissive. Any acknowledgement of inborn psychological differences would be used by men to reserve the most interesting jobs for themselves and tie women once more to the kitchen sink.

Few Feminists would probably go as far as the New York authoress found by an interviewer forcing her young six-year old son to play with dolls. But some Feminist and gay Pagans criticise other branches of Paganism, and especially Wicca, for our emphasis on Goddess-God gender polarity in our rituals.

This strikes most Pagan parents of children of both sexes as ridiculous. We accept that patriarchal society has exaggerated inborn gender differences and sought to make all individuals conform to the 'typical' behaviour of their gender, the peak in the distribution curve of abilities and character. But we know from observing our children that there are natural differences to begin with, without which patriarchal society would have had no opportunity to exaggerate them nor cause to discriminate between men and women.

Equality Both Feminists and Pagans oppose the hierarchical structure of patriarchal society, and have adopted the circle as the form for their meetings, since this gives every participant an equal opportunity to make him or herself heard. But some Feminists go further, and believe that any acknowledgement of differences in skills and abilities between the members of a circle undermines the belief in the equal worth of all members. Behaviour that flaunts a greater ability is regarded in many women's circles as 'oppressive'.

This can lead to an authoritarian levelling of everyone down to the lowest common denominator. To express one's own point of view clearly and succinctly is regarded as oppressive of the less articulate in the group. To dress with taste and make the most of one's appearance is regarded as oppressive of the scruffy and dowdy. Some women's communes have a strict dress code: short hair, slacks, no make-up.

Most other Pagans, and indeed the younger generation of Feminists, would regard such compulsory levelling down as far more oppressive than the competition encouraged by patriarchal society, and impious at the same time. We believe that the Goddess and God have given each of us different inborn abilities with a purpose: that we should thereby need each other, and have something to contribute to each other.

It is not just our right as individuals but our duty to the divine spark within each of us that we feel free to 'do what we will' and develop and exercise our inborn abilities to the full: the articulate to help clarify our thoughts, the creative to enrich our lives with their art, the physically well-endowed to shine with their beauty. We feel that far from giving others complexes, this will encourage them on the contrary to do the same and make the most of their own inborn and acquired skills.

119

The New Age

The New Age is sometimes taken as an umbrella term to cover all the new religious and healing movements that are reacting against contemporary Western materialism, especially those that preach ecological awareness, holistic healing methods, and the benefits of meditation and visualisation. That would include contemporary Paganism. Most Pagans distance ourselves, however, from this common pot into which many observers would throw us, and some even use 'New Age' as a term of abuse, meaning ill-thought-out fuzzy ideas, superficiality when not downright venality. This requires some explanation.

The Religious New Age Some writers on the New Age distinguish between the religious and the secular New Age, but find it difficult to know where to draw the line. Do the recent International Society of Krishna Consciousness and the 100 year old Church of Christ Scientist belong to the religious New Age or not? They would deny it as strenuously as we Pagans do. On the other hand, the late Alice Bailey and Sir George Trevelyan have both used the term 'New Age' in their writings, and would thus appear to define it. The Findhorn Community in Scotland, which most Pagans who have visited it find congenial, is also often regarded as epitomising the religious New Age.

Wherever you draw the line, the New Age contains some antithetical theological ideas. Concepts like the immortality of the soul and the immanence of the divine – to which Pagans hold – rub shoulders with a hierarchy of forms of energy, in which the densest – matter – is a prison of human consciousness from which the latter must gradually free itself (Trevelyan), this last being antithetical to everything Paganism stands for. Human spiritual self-determination, Paganism's guiding principle, contends with guidance from Hidden Masters, channelled entities, and energies reaching us from the Pleiades or the dog star Sirius. Our objection to such ideas is that they make human beings look once more outside themselves for spiritual guidance instead of taking responsibility for ourselves.

The Secular New Age Marilyn Ferguson with her book *The Aquarian Conspiracy* is probably the leading exponent of this tendency. Secular New Agers emphasise that they have no religion, and that the meditation, visualisation and holistic healing methods that they promote can be practised beneficially by the members of all religions and of none. They therefore see Pagans and all forms of New Age religion as extremists who risk antagonising mainstream Christians and Jews, dissuading them from trying these new beneficial techniques by incorporating them in what we contentiously call a new (or a return to the old) religion. Starhawk relates how during a New Age workshop Marilyn Ferguson 'freaked out' at the mention of witchcraft as one of the strands in Aquarian thinking.

Incidentally, the secular New Agers are not alone in this view. Many members of ecological movements, like Greenpeace, Friends of the Earth, etc., are unhappy at Pagans describing themselves as 'the Green Party at prayer'. Raising the religious issue will in their opinion deter Christians, Jews and many agnostics and atheists from supporting ecological causes. Until recently, the organisers of 'Green gatherings' in England refused to allow Pagan groups to put up information tents, while encouraging Christian ecological groups to do so.

This fear has turned out to be unfounded. As organised Paganism has become more visible, the more tolerant and liberal Christian ministers and theologians have taken considerable interest in it, precisely because Paganism presents itself as a religion, which makes it easier for other religious people to understand it. There have been a number of Christian-Pagan meetings and conferences for mutual understanding. At the 1993 Parliament of World Religions in Chicago, Paganism was represented by delegations from the Fellowship of Isis, Circle, the EarthSpirit Community, and the Covenant of the Goddess, whereas no New Age delegations had been invited.

As for the extreme fundamentalist Evangelicals, the non-religious posture of the secular New Age has not pacified them. They tar it with the same 'Satanist' brush as Paganism, non-Christian religions, and – in some cases – the Roman Catholic Church, and have encouraged parents to protest against any teacher who tries to relax his or her class with yoga or meditation techniques.

Pagan Critique of the Secular New Age Pagans see New Agers promoting a new way of life similar to our own, but excluding its very heart by refusing to consider the religious dimension, which normally pulls all the strands of a way of life together. This lack of a religious centre makes New Agers prone to fads and fashions, while rarely considering their implications.

A few years ago, New Agers discovered that rocks, but especially crystals, could be great repositories of energy, in some cases of healing energy. Suddenly, there was a great demand for crystals in New Age shops. To satisfy it, open-cast mining of crystals began in the Ozark and Appalachian mountains in the United States, ruining the ecology of some mountains and valleys hitherto left unscathed by coal mining. There appears also to have been some open-cast mining of crystals in Brazil.

Those who bought crystals in New Age shops rarely had the sensitivity to recognise what energy the crystal they had bought contained: whether it had healing potential and for what diseases, or was useless, or indeed downright harmful. Whatever its energy was, it had probably been stored for the benefit of the mountain or valley from which it had been mined.

A more recent fad has been for Native American religious practices. To exploit this, some half-trained or untrained 'shamans' of mixed Native and white parentage, and some opportunist authors, have run weekend workshops at which they claim to teach the techniques which true Native American medicine men learn in twenty years of often gruelling apprenticeships. For some of these weekend workshops, as much as

$700 per person has been charged in the Los Angeles area. This has led to the common Pagan joke:

> 'What is the difference between Paganism and the New Age?'
> 'One zero in the price of the workshop!'

More seriously, no one who charges this sort of money for a workshop can credibly criticise the destructiveness of contemporary capitalism's exploitative greed: (s)he is part of the same system.

Yet the exploiters represent only a very small proportion of the New Age movement. The vast majority of New Age followers are honest seekers for alternatives to the emptiness of contemporary culture, just like us Pagans. It is time we set aside our mutual suspicions and prejudices, and tried to understand each other better to work together to achieve our common goals.

Tribal Nature Religions

Pagan critique of the faddish superficial New Age interest in Native American religions does not mean that we are not equally interested in them. Our world-view is compatible with that of most tribal religions, whose purpose was to integrate their practitioners with their living environment, and we feel that we have a great deal to learn from them.

We are aware, however, that Native American religions are now the only remaining identifiers of once proud nations, who are acutely resentful of any white attempt to plunder that from them as well. At the above-mentioned 1993 Parliament of World Religions in Chicago, some younger Native American delegates circulated a 'declaration of war' against the New Age for plundering their rituals. So unlike some New Agers, most Pagans would refrain from practising Native American ceremonies unless they had been accepted into a genuine Native American tribe and gone through a full tribal instruction process on a Native American reservation.

North American Pagans are also interested in the many Latin American derivatives from Yoruba orisha worship: Santeria, Voudun and Candomble.

Hinduism

An interest in Eastern religions is regarded as another aspect of the New Age, but it is one that Pagans have fewer reservations in sharing. Many of us have noted similarities between Hinduism and Western Paganism. It appears to be a pantheist religion that sees the divine immanent in Nature and, therefore, in every human and living being, and its concept of *karma* is very close to our experience of the Law of Return. Some white Wiccans and other Pagans therefore also attend their local Hindu temple, have formed friendships and gained valuable insights into their own practice as a result.

The recognition is mutual. A couple of years ago, the journal *Hinduism Today* published a very sympathetic analysis of contemporary Western Paganism, and emphasised all the points common with Hinduism.

Hinduism like Judaism, however, is an ethnic religion, rooted in the Indian sub-continent's history and way of life. The main thing that it shares with Paganism is its diversity of belief and practice, which is even broader than our own. The Shaivite (worshippers of the god Shiva) and Shaktite (worshippers of the Shakti or Life-Force, embodied in the goddess Kali) do indeed emphasise the immanence of the divine and the oneness of Nature. But they also say that most people can only discover the divine in themselves if they first recognise it in their *guru* (master). This runs counter to Western Pagan individualism and sense of spiritual independence.

On the other hand, the Vaishnavites (worshippers of the god Vishnu) are as dualist as Jews and Christians. They see Vishnu as a transcendent power separate from the world, who intervenes occasionally by incarnating as an *avatar*, a divine human being, to help set the world to rights. They see Krishna and Buddha as two such avatars, and are prepared to accept Jesus as having been another one, which is why the oldest

124

branch of Indian Christianity dating from the 2nd century CE is accepted as part of Hinduism.

Just to complicate matters further, the Shaivites – who share our monism – glorify asceticism and the mortification of the flesh, whereas the dualist Vaishnavites share our positive attitude to the enjoyment of life on this earth in an ethical manner.

All branches of Hinduism have goddesses that are the gods' consorts and *shaktis* (energies): Parvati, goddess of Beauty, and Kali, goddess of Death and transformation, as consorts of Shiva; Lakshmi, goddess of wealth, consort of Vishnu, and Sarasvati, goddess of Wisdom and Learning, consort of Brahma. But this doesn't seem to have improved the position of women in Indian society, which is still strongly patriarchal. The belief in karma is also used to buttress the Hindu caste system, a racist product of the Aryan conquest, which leads to particularly cruel attitudes to the 'Untouchable' descendants of the peninsula's original inhabitants.

All this will explain why we don't simply call ourselves *Hindus*.

Taoism

Chinese Taoism (from *tao* meaning the Way) is less complex than Hinduism, and closer to the more mystical side of Western Paganism. Pagans know it mainly from its *yin-yang* polarity, which we often borrow to understand and explain our own polarity between goddess and god energies, though it is not identical.

Buddhism

Many Pagans have taken an interest in Buddhist teachings and sometimes in Buddhist practice in parallel with Pagan rituals. They find Tibetan Buddhist *mandalas* especially meaningful as meditation focuses.

There are no strictures against this from the Buddhist side, one of the world's most tolerant religions, which has co-existed amicably for centuries with tribal religions through-out East and South-East Asia. It is admittedly a somewhat back-handed form of tolerance. According to strict Hinayana (Sri Lanka, Burma, Thailand, Cambodia) Buddhist teaching: 'Gods and goddesses *in as far as they exist at all* are also part of the world of *maya*, and their worship does not therefore lead to liberation. But for people who are not yet ready to be liberated, their worship can be a source of strength and consolation in a world of suffering.'

The Mahayana Buddhism of Tibet, China and Japan is, however, a syncretistic product of Buddhist with indigenous Bon (Tibet) or Taoist (China) pantheistic concepts, and thus far more congenial to contemporary Western Pagans. It allows certain traditional Buddhist concepts to be reinterpreted in a manner that is far more compatible with Pagan convictions.

Maya   The Buddha taught that the material life of the senses on Earth is maya. This is normally interpreted as 'illusion', and therefore as something from which we should liberate our minds as quickly as possible. Euro-American Pagans, on the other hand, delight in the enjoyment of all the physical senses and don't want to let go of them before their natural deaths. The only destructive illusion worth getting rid of is our feeling of *separateness* from our ecological environment and the eternal life-stream.

As Alan Watts, one of the great Western exponents of Zen Buddhism, has pointed out, however, there is an alternative translation of maya: 'game', though the Sanskrit word for this is usually *lilas*. Our physical bodies, our separate personalities, as well as the professional roles we play in human society, are just so many games played by the great Life-Force for its own amusement. We Pagans go along with this, especially when we have become aware of and communicated with the divine spark within ourselves. Our lives and social roles are indeed games, which we can enjoy all the more if we don't take them too seriously nor identify with them.

Non-attachment   If we interpret maya as 'game', then the ideal of non-attachment also becomes more understandable and congenial. It means we should not let ourselves become 'attached' – i.e. identify the essential part of ourselves – to any of the professional or social games we are called upon to play in this life, the better to enjoy them. That is also a Pagan ideal.

Differences arise when we consider human sexual love. In the strictest Buddhist interpretation, this is the greatest and most dangerous form of 'attachment' that ties one to the wheel of *samsara* (reincarnation): to avoid it and attain liberation, Buddhists should therefore live as monks and avoid any sexual intimacy. This is anathema to Pagans for whom love and its sexual component is the greatest joy in life: but then we also look forward to our next incarnation instead of fearing it.

But 'attachment' can also be interpreted as 'possessiveness'. The ideal of non-attachment is then non-possessive love, which respects a loved person's right to love others, and accepts that spiritual growth or one's vocation in this life often lead us in different directions from our loved ones. Non-attachment then allows us to love to the full, enjoy every minute of love, but be prepared to let go of that love when fate demands it: an ideal held by many Pagans.

Reincarnation   Both Buddhists and many though not all Pagans believe that most people reincarnate after death. To Hinayana Buddhists, however, this means an endless round of suffering from which they seek to liberate themselves by achieving *nirvana*. Pagans, on the other hand, delight in life on Earth and the life of the senses and look forward to our next incarnation.

The Mahayana Buddhists, on the other hand, believe that the only thing from which we need to liberate ourselves is *involuntary* reincarnation in a body, family and social role not of our choosing. The Mahayana ideal is the *boddhisattva*, who has achieved liberation from imprisonment in maya, but

127

chooses to postpone his nirvana to reincarnate voluntarily to help others on Earth. Pagans go along with this ideal, especially those Wiccans who believe we know enough about the other side to choose our next incarnation, and to reincarnate in the same time and place as those we have loved in this life.

Nirvana This Buddhist ideal means the dissolution of the separate personality and soul into the eternal life-stream, which is also how many, though not all, Pagans see our ultimate destiny when we have learned all that we needed to learn in our string of incarnations.

Humanism

Humanism and Paganism have so much in common that one might be tempted to regard Paganism as a branch of Humanism. We both reject revealed religion and the unnatural split between *spirit* and *body*, the *sacred* and the *profane*. We both believe in an empirical study of nature, and a pragmatic approach to ethics.

But though our principles are virtually the same, in practice Humanists are often as afraid of their unconscious instincts as Christians, if not more so. They may not regard them as *sinful*, but call them *irrational* which to Humanists is just as bad, especially to their Rationalist wing. As a result, many Humanists give the impression of being as repressed and inhibited as Congregational ministers.

Unitarian Universalism

Whereas the Pagan and New Age ways of life share many practical attitudes but differ in theology, the relationship of Paganism to Unitarian Universalism is the other way around. Our theologies are largely identical but our practice is different.

Unitarians like Pagans reject the Christian dualist opposition of Spirit and Flesh and guidance from Holy Scripture.

Like ourselves Unitarians emphasise human beings' moral autonomy and seek the divine spark – when they are theistic – within rather than outside themselves.

For this reason many Pagans, especially in North America, have also joined the Unitarian Church and have become one of its three leading tendencies, the others being the theists and humanists. They have organised themselves into the Covenant of Unitarian Universalist Pagans (CUUP). Pagans wishing to become full-time religious ministers will normally take a degree from a Unitarian theological college, and then apply to become a Unitarian minister.

But there lies the rub. There are full-time Unitarian ministers precisely because the Unitarian like the Christian churches has a minister–lay congregation model of worship, which brings a host of conservative attitudes in its wake. Like Humanists, Unitarians carry such beliefs as they have in their heads and can be as emotionally repressed as Protestants. A San Francisco Bay area Pagan, who had graduated from the local Unitarian theological college, was sent to a Central Valley parish for a probationary six-month period. They considered her style of dress and worship much too flashy and she was not accepted as a permanent Unitarian minister.

Judaism

Judaism vies with Zoroastrianism for the dubious honour of being the world's first patriarchal monotheist religion. It is certainly the first scriptural religion, and the parent of both Christianity and Islam. As such it would seem cut out to be the prime baddy in Pagan demonology.

But look behind the surface and we find a far more balanced religion than we suspected, especially in Orthodox Judaism. The synagogue may be men's domain, where they alone are allowed to debate the meaning of the Torah, while women sit silently in the gallery. But the Hebrew calendar is lunar and, apart from Passover, their religious festivals are seasonal. Moreover, half if not more of these are celebrated in the home, where the mother of the family reigns supreme, and is given a

129

considerable role in the home-based rituals. Finally, far from demonising sex like the early Christian church, father and mother celebrate the sacred marriage between JHVH and His *shekinah* on the Sabbath night.

Their ritual role in the home gives Jewish women far more self-confidence than Gentile Christian women, so that the leading Feminist writers and the most read American woman writers on Paganism and Wicca are ethnically Jewish. The Reform and Liberal Jewish synagogues now also admit women rabbis.

The balance between male and female elements becomes even more pronounced in the esoteric Kabbalah, with its Tree of Life balanced between male and female *sephiroth* in the two outside pillars. This is admittedly regarded as somewhat subversive by the rabbi establishment, which is why only married Jewish men over the age of 30 are allowed to study it.

There are thus plenty of Pagan elements in Orthodox Judaism for the new Jewish Pagan movement in the United States to focus on. We wish them well in their effort to purify Judaism of its Mosaic or post-Babylonian exile monotheism, and return to the original balance between the male JHVH and His bride Asherah.

Islam

Pagans share the common Western antipathy to contemporary Islamic fundamentalist movements, for their murderous intolerance of dissenters and their repression of women. But scriptural fundamentalism is no more typical of Islam than it is of Judaism or Protestant Christianity: it is just more widespread in contemporary Islamic countries because they are generally poorer than Western countries, and the poor need their faith more to give them self-respect.

A visit to a more prosperous Islamic country like Morocco will show, however, that Islam has many points in common with Paganism. The crescent moon and the five-pointed star are among its symbols, its mosques are often turned toward the setting sun, and their light-promoting architecture includes courtyards filled with flowers, other plants and a fountain. As a desert religion, it has to be ecologically aware, and its critique of the exploitative nature of Western capitalism often echoes Pagan critiques.

This said it remains a bold and unrepentant patriarchal and scripture based religion, and there is no sign of any Islamic Pagan movement. Nor have I met anyone who combines Pagan with Islamic religious practice.

Christianity

In considering Christianity, we have to distinguish between the teachings of the wandering rabbi Jesus of Nazareth nearly 2000 years ago, and those of the churches founded in his name.

No Pagan I know who has studied the teachings of Jesus of Nazareth, or was taught them in his youth, has any quarrel with them. 'He was a great witch!' used to say Gerald Gardner. He despised religious power structures as we do, excoriated the hypocrisy of professional upholders of conventional morality, liked the company of women and treated them as equals, and practised spiritual healing, as do Wiccans and many other Pagan groups.

He tried to teach his listeners to find their own spiritual truth within themselves: 'No one can enter the Kingdom of God except through Me!' (everyone's own Me); and to be spontaneous and open to the wonders of life ('Except ye become as little children, ye cannot enter the Kingdom of God!') Wicca and several other Pagan groups teach the same thing, and try and put it into practice in seasonal festival romps. And he gave initiations to a select group of disciples, including John and Lazarus.

These revolutionary teachings were turned on their head first by Paul and then the Council of Nicaea in what is probably the greatest spiritual fraud in history. Instead of finding the Kingdom of God within our own souls in this life, the churches taught their adherents to find it only after death

131

through faith in the historical Jesus, whose promotion as *only* Son of God implicitly denied everyone else's divinity. Instead of concentrating on Jesus' teachings during his wandering ministry, they morbidly focused on his crucifixion and subsequent believed resurrection.

They thereby turned a message of spiritual liberation into one of social control by existing power structures. The Gnostics, who had continued Jesus' initiatory mystery religion, were suppressed at the end of the 4th century CE. Nonetheless it is the Churches, not Jesus of Nazareth, who have provided the fading Piscean Age's dominant spiritual paradigm, and it is towards them that contemporary Pagans have to adopt some sort of position.

Roman Catholicism and Eastern Orthodoxy

Many Pagans are spiritual refugees from an oppressive Christian upbringing, and view their own former Church, if not all Christian churches, with distaste. Most others simply don't understand the Christian notions of sin and Redemption. Both groups want to leave Christianity well alone, and confine contacts to an effort to remove mutual misconceptions.

A small number of Pagans recognise, however, the Christian God as a cosmic spiritual power equal to – though different from – the Pagan Nature Goddess. They seek to achieve a balance between these two powers in their own lives, by practising both a branch of Paganism and yet remaining members of their Christian church. This was notably the case (at least five to ten years ago) of two well-known women writers: Katherine Kurtz and Caitlin Matthews.

It is probably significant that both of them are women, and that the Christianity they practise(d) is Roman Catholic. Women are temperamentally more inclusive than men, and tend to judge a religion and its rituals more by their feel than the small print of its dogmas. And the Roman Catholic Church is far more of a family than Protestant denominations, and participation in its rituals – notably the Mass – is more

132

important to its practising members than its actual proclaimed beliefs. Moreover, both the Roman Catholic and Eastern Orthodox churches were highly syncretistic of local Pagan practices in their formative centuries.

The Virgin Mary represents a Christianised version of the Pagan triple Goddess: as the Maiden in icons of the Annunciation; as the Mother in the many representations of Her with the infant Jesus on Her lap; as the Crone when, dressed in black, she cradles the dead Jesus' corpse. In Gothic and baroque churches dedicated to Our Lady, her Mother aspect normally dominates the central nave, and her Maiden and Crone aspects the two side transepts. She is often called the Mother of God, in Catholic and Orthodox prayers, and what is the Mother of a God if not a Goddess Herself?

This is, of course, a view that Catholic and Orthodox theologians firmly reject. They place Her above all the saints but well below the Trinity. She may be *venerated* but must on no account be *worshipped*, and Catholics and Orthodox may only pray to Her to intercede on their behalf with Her Son, not to forgive them or grant miracles directly. But go and explain these differences to simple Mediterranean fishermen and farmers, or to inhabitants of the Austrian Alps where there are shrines to Mary at every crossroad.

The right of the Roman Catholic hierarchy to 'interpret' doctrine to the laity is a mechanism allowing commonly accepted popular beliefs to be absorbed into Roman Catholic theology and eventually proclaimed as dogmas, either by Church Councils or more recently by the Pope. Only four new dogmas have been proclaimed since the Council of Trent. Apart from the highly political dogma of the Pope's infallibility in doctrinal matters in 1870 (transferring to the Pope a power previously exercised only by Church councils), all the other three concerned the Virgin Mary. In 1851 her Immaculate Conception (being born without inherited Original Sin) became dogma, and in 1952 her Bodily Assumption likewise. Both had already been believed within the Church for centuries and celebrated with festivals.

The significance of these two dogmas is that Mary has been

acquiring one by one the mythical attributes previously reserved for Her son Jesus Christ, whose Immaculate Conception and Bodily Ascension into Heaven have been the common currency of all Christian churches since at least the Council of Nicaea in 325 CE. Mary's growing importance in Catholic and Orthodox theology thus expresses the slowly rising status of women in Western society after their degradation at the time of the Reformation and the witch hunts.

Since Catholic beliefs tend to arise spontaneously in the laity's collective subconscious long before they are accepted by the hierarchy and proclaimed as dogmas, it is possible for acute observers of the Catholic scene to anticipate future dogmas. Many Catholic poets already refer to Mary as Co-Redemptrix of the human race, thus sharing in the final and most important attribute of Her Son Jesus Christ in Christian theology. And there is also a movement among many Catholic women theologians and nuns – especially in the United States – to see Mary as an incarnation of the third person of the divine Trinity: the Holy Spirit or Sophia seen as female, thus producing a gender-balanced Trinity of Father, Mother and Child.

Mary Magdalene   One aspect of the Pagan Goddess that the Church hierarchy has not allowed the Virgin Mary to absorb is the Aphrodite or Lilith aspect: the Goddess as sexually independent and self-confident seducer. Not surprisingly, given the sexual phobias of the celibate Catholic clergy! But popular myth has filled the gap with highly unscriptural beliefs about Mary Magdalene, one of three Marys weeping at the foot of the Cross.

She was probably Jesus' wife, since no Jew of 30 or over would have been accepted as *rabbi* (teacher) if he wasn't married. But she has also been conflated with the 'sinful woman' who bathed Jesus' feet with her tears and perfumed oils, and of whom Jesus said: 'She has loved much, so much will be forgiven her!'

The popular conflation of Jesus' wife with a (repentant) prostitute in the single person of Mary Magdalene is the direct

134

descendant of the Middle Eastern Pagan fertility myth. The crucified Jesus takes over from the sacrificed Attis or vegetation god as husband or lover of the fertility Goddess who becomes Mary Magdalene. Many churches dedicated to Mary Magdalene were probably once temples of Aphrodite and are places of tremendous power, notably the one on top of the hill at Vezelay in Burgundy.

Saints Many saints presiding over sacred wells, or to whose images found in certain churches miraculous healing powers are attributed, are probably Christianised versions of elemental spirits and guardians of power spots in the countryside, on top of which churches were built.

Pagan and New Age ideas among Roman Catholics

Roman Catholic syncretism means that ideas regarded as Pagan in northern Europe and North America are making their way in Catholic southern Europe within the Church's broad bosom. I moved to Austria three years ago, where 83 per cent of the population still regard themselves as Roman Catholic. There is no organised Pagan movement, and only one or two Wiccan covens in or around Vienna. But the New Age is well represented and esoteric fairs well attended.

There is a growing interest not only in ecological protection, but in geomancy (becoming sensitive to elemental nature spirits – all the easier when some of them were turned into saints centuries ago); Celtic stone circles and other power spots in the countryside, balancing its energies, and guided meditations and path workings; in addition to the usual interest in astrology, Tarot reading, and crystals. Even references to the Triple Earth Goddess in geomantic workshops cause no stir. We should not, therefore, let different labels act as barriers to understanding: a return to Nature reverence, even under a Roman Catholic label, can be just as effective and desirable.

While geomancy, astrology and Tarot reading are still

minority interests in Austria, as is northern European, North American and Australian Paganism, belief in the immanence rather than transcendence of God is gaining ground throughout the younger generation. A growing number of priests and Protestant ministers are as disenchanted as Pagans with the blind materialist acquisitive society that monotheist dualism and transcendentalism has fathered. So they emphasise God's *immanence* in His creation in their sermons, though to cover their backs they call in *panentheism* (God is in the world but more than the world) rather than pantheism. They also acknowledge every individual's right to find his or her own direct channel to God: they are there just to help when needed. No Druid or Wiccan could put it better!

Despite his expulsion from the Dominican order and the Catholic Church, Matthew Fox's *Creation Spirituality* continues to make headway in the spiritual underground of both the Catholic and many Protestant churches. This emphasises the *Original Blessing* of life itself instead of the 'Original Sin' of having animal instincts and lusts that our reason cannot always adequately control.

Recent attempts by the Vatican to reimpose a more traditional hierarchical concept of the priesthood – by appointing very hardline conservative bishops and archbishop – have resulted in a Catholic People's Petition (Volksbegehren) signed by over 500,000 practising Catholics (out of 3.5 million) in June 1995, requesting:

1. Equal recognition of the laity as full members of the Church with a right to be heard.
2. Lay and parish priest participation in the election of bishops.
3. The right of priests to marry, thus freeing them from the temptation to abuse their women parishioners and children sexually.
4. Equal access for women to all positions in the Church hierarchy.
5. Greater emphasis on the glad tidings in the Christian message than on threats of damnation to sinners.

136

Nonetheless, Roman Catholic, like all Christian religious ceremonies contain certain statements that the congregation recites together with the officiating priest. Their effect at the unconscious level is all the greater when participants just repeat them mechanically without thinking about them. And in two cases, at least these run diametrically counter to everything that Paganism stands for.

The General Confession of Sins

I don't know the exact words used in the Roman Catholic Church, but in the Anglican church – whose rituals are based on original Roman Catholic ones – they ran as follows 40 years ago:

> We readily acknowledge our manifold sins and wicked-
> nesses.
> We have done that which we should not have done, and
> We have not done that which we should have done
> And there is no hope for us!

Repeated Sunday after Sunday, it induces a sense of moral impotence and unworthiness in all the participants, which is the whole aim of the operation: that they should feel morally helpless without the Church. The failure of so many practising Christians to live up to their proclaimed ideals of neighbourly love may well be due to the fact that they are living *down* to the General Confession of Sins' expectations.

This has admittedly been toned down in the more recent Anglican Alternative Service Book to read as follows:

> Almighty God, our heavenly Father, we have sinned against you and against our fellow men, in thought and word and deed, through negligence, through weakness, through our own deliberate fault. We are truly sorry and repent of all our sins. For the sake of your Son Jesus Christ, who died for us, forgive us all that is past, and grant that we may serve you in newness of life to the glory of your name. Amen.

137

This still runs directly counter to the Pagan conviction that we are all essentially divine, and that we each have the capacity to live and behave like god(desse)s. What is the point in practising Pagan rituals that build us up, if we then go the next Sunday to confess in common our moral impotence and unworthiness? Anyone who believes in the words of the General Confession of Sins is no Pagan; anyone who doesn't probably wouldn't be recognised as a Christian, since without common moral helplessness and sinfulness there is no point in the Redemption.

The Nicene, or Apostles', Creed

This is recited by the whole Anglican or Roman Catholic congregation at the end of each religious service. Here is the King James version with which I am familiar:

I believe in One God, the Father Almighty, Creator of Heaven and Earth and of all things both visible and invisible.

And I believe in Jesus-Christ, His only begotten Son, Who was born of a Virgin, was crucified, dead and buried and descended into Hell. On the third day He rose again, and now sitteth on the Right Hand of the Father Almighty, from whence He shall return on the last day to judge the quick and the dead.

And I believe in one Holy Catholic Church, the communion of saints, the forgiveness of sins, and life everlasting.

Now let us deconstruct this statement of belief to see how far it is compatible with Pagan pantheist convictions.

'I believe in *One God*.' If it stood by itself, it would be ambiguous. It could be an *inclusive* statement of the unity of all creation, with which Pagans would certainly agree. Or it could be an *exclusive* statement, denying the existence of any other god(esse)s.

The next part of the sentence makes it quite clear that it is indeed an *exclusive* statement: 'the *Father* Almighty' thereby explicitly excluding the belief in any *Mother* Goddess; '*Creator of Heaven and Earth and all things visible and invisible*', thereby implicitly denying the divinity of the created Universe itself.

'And I believe in Jesus Christ, His *only begotten Son*' This implicitly denies the divinity of any other human being who has ever lived, let alone of other non-human living beings, which is the cornerstone of Pagan convictions.

'Who was born of a *Virgin*.' Just what does that mean? In Aramaic – the language that Jesus of Nazareth and his disciples spoke – a virgin means apparently a woman who has not yet had her first child. That would simply mean that Jesus was the eldest of Mary's children, which would be irrelevant to the validity of his message. In Latin, it means an unmarried woman, which would make Jesus a bastard, hardly the image the Church wants to convey.

No, what the bishops assembled at Nicaea in 325 CE meant, of course, was that Jesus was born of a *virgo intacta* by parthenogenesis, having been conceived without human sexual intercourse. The implication is that sexual intercourse – to Pagans the supreme sacrament, a gateway to self-transcendence into communion with the divine – is so defiling that no true Son of God could conceivably be conceived in that manner! Anybody who believes that, or even just affirms that belief, is no Pagan and has no right to participate in Pagan fertility festivals.

'Who was crucified, dead and buried, and descended into Hell. On the third day, He rose again, and now sitteth on the Right Hand of the Father Almighty, from whence He shall return on the last day, to judge the quick and the dead.

'And I believe in One Holy Catholic Church, the communion of saints, the forgiveness of sins and life everlasting.'

These last statements all hang together. By accepting to be crucified, Jesus Christ took upon Himself the sins of the world and redeemed them. We can avail ourselves of this Redemption, have our sins forgiven and attain life everlasting if we belong to the One Holy Catholic Church and thereby participate in the 'communion of saints'. Otherwise we shall be judged on the last day.

No true Pagan can believe any of this and still be a Pagan. To be a Pagan means to be conscious of our own divinity, and to take responsibility for our actions. If we wrong someone, we have to make it up to them in this life or the next, and no Jewish preacher, however good and charismatic, can relieve us of our personal responsibility in this respect. We all enjoy life everlasting without membership of any church, initially as souls reborn through a cycle of incarnations (as many though not all Pagans believe), eventually as part of the eternal life-stream. But whether on this Earth or on a more spiritual plane, our future lives will be as full of challenges as this one, because that is the nature of the games that the Life-Force plays!

How many Christians actually believe in every article of the Apostles' Creed? A moot point. Apparently not all Anglican bishops do, but that is no reason for Pagans wishing to build bridges with Christians to participate in reciting such an offensive creed. To proclaim beliefs that one does not hold is, according to Jesus, to commit the 'sin against the Holy Spirit.'

Protestant Christianity

The various Protestant churches are quite different from Roman Catholicism and Eastern Orthodoxy. They threw out all the syncretised Pagan elements from their beliefs and rituals at the time of the Reformation, and have thus made their brand of Christianity the purest form of patriarchal monotheism. It is entirely Scripture-based and intellectual, and makes no concessions to the emotions.

There are thus no common elements of belief that Pagans would recognise: so unsurprisingly, we have had to create a Pagan movement outside the churches in the Protestant dominated countries. But let us not forget our debt to Protestant individualism for giving us the self-assurance to trust our own experiences.

And yet, Protestantism too is changing. It is paradoxical that it is in the historically Protestant countries – where there is no feminine deity or proto-deity at all – that the status of women has risen fastest, and that the Protestant churches are so far the only ones to have admitted women to their ministry. They are admittedly 'women ministers' or 'women priests' not priestesses, and thus expected to preach in a male deductive mode. But even so, what will their effect be on Protestant church practice in a couple of generations?

Then we have the charismatic 'happy clappy' Evangelical movement, with a very Dionysian appeal to the emotions, and with a growing interest in spiritual healing: not all that unlike what goes on at Pagan seasonal festivals and gatherings. As churches are emptying of their congregations, 'house churches' not unlike Wiccan covens and Druid groves are said to be proliferating.

The Earth Goddess' energy is rising in the collective unconscious of Western society, and She is no respecter of confessional boundaries!

Summary

In the last seven chapters I have tried to show that the best way to prevent Western society from destroying the Earth's ecology irretrievably is to re-integrate human consciousness with Nature consciousness, so that we see ourselves once more as *part* of Nature instead of standing outside it. The best means to do so is a return to the pantheist polytheist religious paradigm of our ancestors, which recognises the divine as *immanent* in all human beings, women as well as men, animals and plants; and recognises the feminine quality of Being and loving as equally divine as the masculine quality of doing.

Contemporary Western Paganism represents this paradigm in its pure form, and it is spreading primarily in formerly Protestant countries by a process of radical displacement of the older patriarchal monotheist paradigm. But the paradigm of immanence is also spreading by a process of syncretism within the Roman Catholic church laity and through some theologians in predominantly Catholic countries.

SUMMARY TABLE of CHARACTERISTICS

	Christianity	Paganism
Sources of truth	The Bible + Church	Personal experience
Conception of the divine	Transcendent	Immanent in life
Personal deities	One in 3 persons: Father, Son, Holy Spirit	Two or more: Goddess, Horned God + multiple ethnic deities in several traditions
Other helpers	In Roman Catholicism and Eastern Orthodoxy: Virgin Mary, saints	Guardians of quarters, Elemental spirits
Pattern of worship	Priest–congregation	Circle of equals
Place of worship	Consecrated church	Out of doors, or home
Festivals celebrate	Historical episodes in life of Jesus	Seasons of the year
Concept of human nature	Fallen, in need of Redemption	Divine
Humanity's relationship to Nature	External	Part of it
Attitude to science	Guarded: separate realm	Positive, but rejects materialist dogma
Environmental control	Rational, technological	Rational, technical and magical
Concept of history	Linear	Circular
Ethics	Deductive and prescriptive	Pragmatic
Spiritual ideal	Salvation in the next world through faith in Jesus Christ	Self-realisation in this life in harmony with Nature and the cosmos

143

III

Handling Power

11

An Initiatory Path

Most religions have some initiatory orders, whose members devote themselves to serve their deities as the centre of their lives, as well as to understand the deeper 'occult' (=hidden) currents underneath surface appearances. They are the Roman Catholic and Orthodox Christian monastic orders, the Muslim Sufis, the Hindu Tantrics and Vedantists.

Modern Paganism is no different. There are a number of initiatory traditions within it, of which the best known are the Pagan Druid orders and Wicca. (Not all Druid orders are Pagan or even religious. The Ancient Order of Druids is a purely social organisation, while the Welsh Gorsedd is Celtic nationalist and counts many Christian ministers among its leading members.) The equally initiatory Ordo Templis Orientis (OTO) and the Chaos magicians of the Illuminati of Thanateros (IOT) are also usually counted as Pagan, although they are solely concerned with the self-empowerment of their members and not with Nature worship. As I am a Wiccan, I will try and explain its aims and practice, leaving the members of other esoteric Pagan traditions to speak for themselves.

Wiccan Origins

Wicca is the Anglo-Saxon word from whose plural *wicce* (pronounced *witche*) the modern English word *witch* is derived. In the 1950s and 1960s its members simply called themselves *witches*, and in America *witchcraft* and *Wicca* are still used as synonyms. This has the disadvantage, however, that *witch* and *witchcraft* are generic words, commonly used to describe village wise women and cunning men who mostly work on their own and have usually learned their craft within the family. It cannot, therefore, be appropriated by an initiatory tradition, even when this practises the same types of spiritual healing and spellcasting techniques as country witches. Hence the English practice of distinguishing initiatory *Wicca* from ordinary country *witchcraft*.

Like most magical orders initiatory Wicca aims to further our initiates' spiritual development, and help us to recognise and then act on our own true will; but it aims to do so within a framework of harmony with Nature. In order to open up our imaginations and channels of communication between our conscious and unconscious levels of the mind, we use magical rituals derived from Co-Masonry (a form of Freemasonry that admits both men and women), the Golden Dawn and – through them – Renaissance magic and Egyptian temple magic of 2000 to 5000 years ago. We also learn and practise country spellcasting techniques, which we use for spiritual healing and helping our members and friends.

Until the 1950s Wicca was, like all magical orders of the time a very secretive tradition known only to its few members. Gerald Gardner first publicised it with his books *Witchcraft Today* (1954) and *The Meaning of Witchcraft* (1959), since when its membership has grown exponentially in the English-speaking countries and, more recently, in other northern European Protestant countries.

Wicca owes its popularity partly to the fact that until the early 1970s it was the only organised form of Goddess worship. Many people, especially in Britain and Germany, still regard it as a religion in its own right. But we no longer reserve our theology, such as it is, or our purely religious seasonal festivals to our initiated members, but share them with the wider Pagan community: they were described in the previous part of this book. Only our magical techniques remain secret and reserved to our initiates.

A Chthonic Magical Tradition

Wiccans help ourselves and others with *witchcraft*: a set of mental and spiritual techniques for developing the power of the mind to communicate consciously with our own subconscious, and through it with the collective unconscious of the human race and ultimately the whole of life, including the cosmic and chthonic energies we call Goddess(es) and God(s). Mastering these techniques allows initiates to affect our own state of mind and of physical health as well as those of anyone we know with their consent, our and other people's fate and chances in life, and even the weather. In the next chapter, I give a few case histories to show just how effective these techniques can be.

Like drugs, the effectiveness of these mental and spiritual techniques is directly proportionate to their danger to the practitioner's sanity. While it is possible to become an effective solo magician just by reading DIY magical books, it is also very conducive to ego-inflation, delusions of grandeur or, on the contrary, paranoia and even demonic possession. (A 'demon' in this context is a destructive energy, such as an addiction, or a thought-form projected by a repressed, frustrated or schizophrenic person.)

That is why Wiccans only learn to practise magic within our covens, in which we use tried and proven protective techniques, and members can keep an informal eye on each other's state of mind and rescue those who get into deeper psychic waters than they can cope with. The covens in turn will only admit new members whom they like and can trust not to misuse for unethical ends the techniques they will be taught.

All this is common ground to all magical traditions. Where Wicca differs from the Druids and the various orders of the so-called 'Western Mysteries' is in the energies that we use in our magical work. Most other magical orders work mainly with *celestial* or *solar* energy that reaches us through our heads. They thus wear magical robes, that are sufficiently different from street clothes to make the participants feel part of an altered reality, but nonetheless cover the whole body except the head.

Wiccans, on the contrary, work as much with *lunar* energy that stimulates the imagination, and with the *chthonic* energy of the Earth and our physical bodies. We thus work naked whenever we can in secluded spots out of doors during the summer months, and indoors during the cold weather. Nakedness allows us to exchange energy with our living surroundings through every pore of our bodies and not just our heads, and induces a feeling of unity with the life-stream that has to be experienced to be understood. (Nude swimming and sunbathing can have the same effect.)

Energetic round dancing to raise energy also plays an important part in Wiccan magical work, which is also much easier and more effective if one is unimpeded by any clothes. In this respect, Wicca has more in common with African and other tribal forms of magic than with other Western mystery traditions.

Why the Secrecy?

Secrecy is part of a coven's protective wall. It helps us experience a mysterious altered reality within our magical circles. It acts also as a constraint for the energy we raise and project in our work to make it effective.

Just as steam or gasoline gases can only drive engines by being constrained into a cylinder, so the power of the human mind can only affect its environment if it too is constrained through intense focusing; the boundaries of a magical circle; and strict secrecy, not only about the techniques used but the purpose sought. Any discussion of a spell after it has been cast, especially outside the circle where it was cast, dissipates its energy and thus lessens the chances of its object being achieved.

We also keep our magical techniques secret from non-initiates so that no one outside a Wiccan coven be tempted to try them out without our protective mechanisms.

All forms of magic challenge the Western materialist paradigm that we can only act on our environment with our hands and speech: they thus induce fear among people whose sense of security is bound up with this paradigm. Wicca goes further by deliberately defying the sense of shame about our bodies that the patriarchal religions promote, which lays us open to the prurient speculations of the gutter press. A great deal of hostility from conventional society is thus to be expected. Secrecy – especially about the identity of our fellow members – is thus an elementary defence.

The Three Degree Paradigm

There are three degrees of initiation in Wicca, as in most Freemason lodges, who in turn took this system over from the mediaeval craft guilds. Indeed, like the Freemasons, we Wiccans tend to call our tradition 'the Craft' among ourselves. The craft guilds governed all trades and early industry for centuries. Their three degree system is thus a very powerful paradigm, which we must understand to work it effectively, even though the three Wiccan degrees also differ in some important respects.

In the Middle Ages, when a boy (it usually was a boy) wanted to become say, a baker, his parents would approach a master baker in the same city and ask him to take him on as apprentice. If the master baker accepted, then at 14 the boy would leave his parents' home and move into the master baker's house and become to all intents and purposes a member of his family. He would have to obey the master in all things and watch him at work at all the hours when this was necessary, including getting up at 4 a.m. to light the ovens to bake the bread that customers would be buying fresh from 7 a.m. onwards; or serving in the shop.

As the young apprentice learned the craft of bread baking, he would be gradually entrusted with smaller and then bigger tasks. At first, it might be just serving in the shop. Later, he might be trusted to bake the morning bread on his own. Finally, he would be taught how to buy different types of flour, how to recognise good from bad, how to haggle about the price.

When the master baker regarded his young apprentice as fully competent in all that he could teach him, he would formally raise him to the status of companion or journeyman baker, usually between the ages of 18 and 21. He would now be entitled to be paid a wage for his work in the bakery. Mostly, however, he would now leave his master's employ and travel to other cities, sometimes to other countries throughout Europe. In each city he visited, he would seek work with a local master baker, and learn his way of baking bread and cakes, which would vary from city to city and, of course, from country to country as it still does today.

After ten to twelve years' travelling in this way, when the journeyman baker felt he had learned all he could about the art of baking bread throughout England or Europe, he would return to the city of his birth and the bakery where he had first learned his trade. There, under the guidance of his original master, he would in his spare time work on his *masterpiece*: the most artistic and tasty loaf of bread or cake that he was capable of making. At the next bakers' guild festival, he would present his masterpiece to all the assembled master bakers of the city.

If the masterpiece passed muster, its author would then be ceremoniously raised to the status of master baker. He would now be entitled to marry – frequently the daughter of his original master – to open his own baker's shop, employ journeymen and take on apprentices of his own.

Wiccan initiation and the two subsequent elevations to the Second and Third degrees usually follow this paradigm fairly closely. The main differences are that men and women are initiated equally, and are always a great deal older at their first degree initiation: the minimum age is 18.

The First (Apprentice) Degree

Pagans who feel a vocation to become Wiccans have to approach the 'High Priestess' of a working coven and ask for initiation: no easy task as most high priestesses keep their coven identity and their own role in it secret. But active participation in open Pagan seasonal festivals and other events increases their chances of making the right friendships and being spotted.

A year and a day Until a decade ago, at least a year and a day had to elapse between the initial request and the initiation: enough time for all the existing members of the coven to get to know the postulant, find out whether they liked her or him, and test her/his seriousness by seeing whether (s)he was still as keen a year later, or if it had been merely a passing whim.

A year and a day also represents a complete cycle of the seasons. The postulant would be asked to observe closely this cycle in a wood or meadow close to her/his home, get acquainted with its trees, bushes and little animals and how they behave in each season, and thus put Wicca firmly into its Nature-worshipping context.

Today, a postulant is often already quite well known by the members of the coven (s)he wishes to enter through common participation in open seasonal festivals, open discussion groups and pub moots. If (s)he has then shown considerable familiarity with Nature and the seasonal cycle, the probationary period can be kept much shorter. It can also be shortened for postulants whom the coven members feel to have a natural ability for witchcraft: I had only to wait four months from the date I first met Gerald Gardner.

Most covens also give some pre-initiatory training to their postulants these days: in Wicca's and the coven's spiritual principles, and basic inner working techniques. Beside preparing them for initiation, it also allows them to check whether Wicca is the right path, and this coven the right one for them.

Healing the crippled psyche

Wicca assumes that most postulants will have been influenced by society's mores, and quite frequently repressed into conformity with them. These repress men's emotional side and boost their aggressive assertiveness, while they repress women's assertiveness and encourage them to be meek and submissive in a 'feminine' way.

Each gender is thus crippled differently by society, and has to learn from the other gender what (s)he is missing in their character. This is symbolised by the Wiccan practice of cross-gender initiation. Male postulants are thus always initiated by the High Priestess: they are thus put on notice that they will have a lot to learn from the women in the group, notably to be more tolerant and intuitive, and are 'plugged' magically into the strong but gentle Goddess current.

Women postulants are initiated by the High Priest and 'plugged' into the Horned God current, which will help them in time to gain in self-confidence and assertiveness.

As men and women initiates become less repressed and more balanced between the receptive and assertive parts of our character, they also gain in self confidence to follow their true wills, irrespective of social pressures.

Initiation

The initiation itself will normally take place at the time of one of the major Pagan festivals, but obviously in a closed meeting attended only by the other coven members. The ceremony is structured ritually and psychologically as a rite of rebirth, in which the initiate is reborn into the family of the coven, but at the same also into the world wide family of Wiccans who are all 'plugged in' to the Goddess and God current.

The oath of secrecy is a very important part of the proceedings. It makes the initiate aware of the wall of secrecy and mystery surrounding the coven, allowing all to work with the Goddess and God currents. It also allows each member to open up her/his feelings to the coven in a way (s)he would never do in the outside world, and be prepared to learn more about the inner life of other coven members than (s)he would normally learn about anyone but a close family member or a spouse. Such close mutual trust would obviously be destroyed if anyone felt their innermost confidences might become the subject of bar-room gossip outside the coven.

Towards the end of the initiation, the initiate is proclaimed 'Priest(ess) and Witch', to indicate that (s)he is considered from the beginning an equal member of the coven, with equal access to the Goddess and God current.

Psychological growth

The initiation will generally accelerate the new Wiccan's psychological and emotional growth. (S)he may have to confront painful repressed memories from her/his past, as a prelude to purging them and growing beyond them. This can be a painful and frightening process, which the initiate should be able to discuss with an experienced person, but few if any people outside Wicca would understand what is going on.

This is where the family feeling of the typical Wiccan coven becomes so important, as well as the strong emotional bonds that a properly handled initiation normally weaves between the initiate and her/his initiator. It is vital that at this time the initiate should feel confident of being able to attend every coven meeting as of right, and if possible have access to her/his initiator between meetings if a psychological crisis should arise.

These warm bonds between coven members with each other and their High Priest(ess) attract many lonely people to Wicca in our vast impersonal cities, and create an ever growing demand for Wiccan initiations. Faced with this, a few Wiccan High Priest(esse)s have initiated far more postulants than they can fit into their regular coven, or whose psychological progress they have the time to follow closely. They then invite them to attend the odd seasonal festival on an irregular basis. They doubtless feel that even though they cannot offer them regular coven membership, at least they can plug them into the

155

Wiccan current and put them in touch with the Goddess and the God.

Although well-meant, the effect on the semi-abandoned initiates has sometimes been devastating: it is as if, after being reborn psychologically, they have been dumped on the street to fend for themselves. Wiccans will therefore generally advise seekers to follow their instincts, and apply only to groups whose members they have all met, that have a positive and balanced feel to them, and to make sure they will actually be part of a coven if initiated.

Coven Activities

During their apprenticeship, Wiccan initiates learn by participating in coven meetings the techniques for psychic protection, raising power and projecting it, the rituals performed during the course of a year, and their symbolic significance.

Some covens use always the same traditional words for each ritual, because of the *morphic resonance* these have acquired by being used thousands of times around the world for decades: First degree initiates will have to memorise these. Others feel it more effective to use new words each time: initiates then learn how to improvise words that are true to the ritual's symbolism.

Most covens also encourage their First degree initiates to acquire a specialised area of knowledge appropriate to their temperament. Those with psychic abilities will be encouraged to learn some traditional divination technique, such as scrying, Tarot reading and/or casting astrological horoscopes. Greenfingered initiates will be encouraged to develop their herbal knowledge. More extrovert initiates may be encouraged to develop their organising ability by planning and running an open seasonal festival for the local Pagan community.

The Second (Companion) Degree

When the apprentice has learned all the coven's magical techniques, the special skill (s)he has chosen, and fulfilled all the other coven requirements, (s)he will be raised to the second degree at her or his request and with the High Priestess's and High Priest's consent.

This takes the form of a new initiatory ritual, in which the postulant is taken on a journey into the underworld and taught the significance of the life-cycle. (S)he also dedicates her or himself to being a proper channel for the Goddess and the God, after being warned that this may involve a painful purification of her/his being of all those elements unworthy of these pure energies.

The impact of this elevation ritual varies from person to person, but it frequently becomes apparent not at the time of the ritual but in the person's life days, weeks or months after the ritual itself. In my case, I did not feel any greater contact with the Goddess and God current during the elevation ritual than I had felt at my initiation and in subsequent coven meetings, though I found the descent into the underworld very beautiful and poetic. But two days after the elevation ritual, I had the mystical experience of cosmic consciousness that I described in the first chapter.

Others have sometimes entered 'the dark night of the soul' after their Second degree elevation, becoming suddenly far more conscious of inadequacies in their own character or of the relationship which they are in, or the unsuitability of their civilian job. When that happens, coven support is once more essential.

After the elevation, the new Second degree companion will be trusted to manage not only her/his own energy, but if need be the coven's collective energy. As such (s)he will know enough to deputise for the High Priest(ess) at a meeting, usually at first in the High Priest(ess)'s presence who will be able to encourage the companion and help out if her/his confidence should desert her/him.

In recent years, many Second degree companions have also

gone on training courses outside the coven in counselling, individual and group therapy as useful skills in coven leadership, and to make themselves available as priest(esse)s to the wider Pagan community.

Apart from that, Second degree Wiccans continue to attend their coven's meetings as they did when they were apprentices.

Journeying

Some covens have, however, borrowed from mediaeval practice and encourage their Second degree companions to accept invitations from other covens to attend their meetings as guests or even as full-time members for a while and learn their techniques.

During the last ten years my professional life has taken me to California at least once a year. During these visits, I have often been invited as a guest by local Wiccan covens or Church of All Worlds nests, and have learned a great deal from them. Whereas my London coven is expert at spiritual healing, it wasn't until I participated in Californian circles that I learned how simple weather magic can be, as I shall show in the next chapter.

I must emphasise, however, that membership of one Wiccan coven, whether as apprentice or companion, gives no one an automatic right to attend another coven's meetings. (S)he has to be invited, and will only be invited if her/his character and temperament are compatible with the host coven. Mutual liking and trust between coven members is an absolute essential for effective coven work and magic.

12

Do Spells Work?

In 1983 Tanya Luhrmann, an American anthropologist, was initiated into my coven as part of her field work on the London magical and witchcraft community for her Ph.D. thesis at Cambridge University. She submitted this (*Scions of Prospero*) to the university in 1986, and then turned it into a book *Persuasions of the Witch's Craft*, which was published in 1989.

Dr Luhrmann gave us plenty of good marks. We are no *cult*, as commonly understood, since we have no authoritarian head and no one makes any money out of us. We are neither feeble-minded nor social drop-outs, since many of us work in industry and commerce, with a particular emphasis on the computer industry. Our magical training techniques appear to be very therapeutic in developing our imaginations, and make us above average at the jobs we do. And Wiccan coven organisation gives us a comforting sense of community which is all too often lacking in contemporary society.

On one point, however, Dr Luhrmann felt she had to draw the line: the efficacy of instrumental magic, i.e. the ability to influence other people's health, the weather and events in general by the power of the focused mind alone. Indeed, she wrote into her Introduction that she herself did not believe in the power of magical spells.

Having thus adopted the conventionally sceptical attitude,

Dr Luhrmann then faced the problem of why apparently intelligent, educated and professionally effective people could believe in magical efficacy and thus share a mindset that previous anthropological authorities – notably Sir James Fraser and Evans-Wentz – had characterised as typical only of pre-civilised, pre-scientific tribal peoples. Her conclusion was the *Interpretive Drift*: just as lawyers who socialise mainly with other lawyers think and speak as lawyers, and computer people have their own language understood only by themselves, so witches and magicians who consort socially mainly with other witches and magicians tend in time to take all the magical community's assumptions for granted.

'The only reason I did not was that I had a very strong disincentive to do so. I stood to lose both credibility and my career...' she wrote in a revealing passage. And there is no reason to doubt her assessment of her academic colleagues. Did not one of them write that it was the duty of universities to 'build a bulwark against the rising tide of irrationalism'.

Nor is scepticism about the efficacy of instrumental magic confined to the academic and scientific community. In 1989 the American Pagan magazine *Fire Heart* published a round-table discussion on magical ethics. Out of four American Pagans asked to contribute, three did not address the issue, because they thought spells only affect the state of mind of the person working them.

These prejudices are easy to understand. The concept that we can influence other people and even events by the power of our minds alone strikes at the root of the materialist scientific paradigm on which the whole of modern science and technology is based.

The Theoretical Basis of Magic and Spells

Given this scepticism and downright hostility, a brief theoretical explanation of why magic and spells might work is in order. Quantum physics shows that everything in the universe – including ourselves – is energy at different frequency levels. It has also found that two particles that have once come into contact thereafter react identically, often simultaneously down to the nanosecond, despite being physically separated. Everything in the universe is therefore connected at the energy level, and any form of energy can influence other forms of energy, either through direct contact, or remotely if they have previously been in contact.

The electronic industry exploits these properties of energy. Sounds emitted in a concert hall or a studio can be turned into invisible radio waves, which radio sets on the same frequency distributed over thousands of miles can turn back into the same sound virtually instantaneously. Dramas performed in a studio or street scenes captured by a news camera can similarly be turned into invisible high-frequency waves to be turned back into the same moving pictures by television sets distributed over hundreds of miles. Why, with all this daily experience of radio and television around us, it should still be regarded as impossible for human thoughts to be transmitted in a similar manner has always puzzled me.

They can, however, and magic is the art of making this happen effectively. It requires the absolute conviction on the part of the practitioner(s) that (s)he/they is/are an energy form connected to all other energies of the universe; an ability to focus thoughts, and a strong emotional will to achieve the desired results. The person being influenced does not have to believe in magic nor even to know that (s)he is being worked on, though it helps.

The chances of its working depend on the balance between the psychic energy of the magician(s) or witch(es) doing the willing and the energy that needs to be influenced, and how closely the two are related. A solo magician trying to influence the actions of a foreign government, none of whose members (s)he has ever met, has fewer chances of success than a coven of witches trying to heal or find a job for one of their members or friends whom they know well and to whom they are bound by close affectionate ties.

Success does not always have to depend on the personal energy that the magician(s) or witch(es) can muster. Just as telephone signals and televisual images can sometimes be transmitted over long distances more cheaply by being beamed up to and bounced off a satellite than by terrestrial cable, the most effective spells are those in which we enlist the Goddess's or the God's cosmic energy to aid us instead of trying to do it all ourselves. In this way, we can sometimes cause 'ripples in the web of fate' of those we are trying to help.

Validating the Efficacy of Spells

Dr Luhrmann was wrong, however, to say that it is mainly the company of other witches and magicians that makes us believe in the efficacy of magical spells. We do so because the desired results are achieved more often than not within a comparatively short time of the spell.

None of us have, however, ever tried to suspend the laws of physics or of nature in general. We are not in the Jesus of Nazareth class: able to walk on water, make blind people see, lame people walk and even cure people unawares if they but touched him behind his back. The most we can claim for our spells is that they make the *possible* we wish *probable*, sooner rather than later.

This gives determined sceptics the possibility of claiming that 'it might have happened anyway', and that our healings rely wholly on the placebo effect. What they fail to take into consideration is the time dimension. A person out of a job for a year before asking us for a spell might have found a job by her/himself at any time during those twelve months but didn't. (S)he might have found a job without our help at any time during the next year or two. But when (s)he finds a job within a month of us working a spell for her/him, then we feel justified in thinking our spell might have had something to do with the result.

In considering this argument Dr Luhrmann complained that all she was ever offered when discussing instrumental magic was anecdotal evidence rather than statistics of successful versus unsuccessful spells. I gave her a list of the nine most dramatically successful spells that I could remember: not much to show, she wrote, for 30 years of coven work!

This misses the point. To prove the possibility of mechanical flight, the Wright brothers did not have to make *Kitty Hawk* take off every time; they had to make her take off just once even if only for a few hundred yards. Brought up in a materialist scientific culture that is uniquely hostile to instrumental magic, with no family history of magical practice behind us as tribal shamans normally possess, we are in magic where the Wright brothers were in manned mechanical flight. It is a wonder that our spells ever work, let alone work as often and as dramatically as they have done. Statistics of successful spells would only become relevant if any of us were to set up as professional faith-healers.

Here then are a few of the successful spells that I can remember from 40 years of Wiccan practice. I emphasise these are not the only successful spells of that period, just the more dramatic ones that I can remember. I will include some from other religions' practitioners. In evaluating them as evidence, let the reader not forget the time dimension. What were the chances not just of the desired results happening, but of happening within the time-scale that they did?

The Interrupted Cold

In September 1979 I was visiting my mother-in-law, a Christian Science practitioner (healer), with my then wife when I felt the unmistakable signs of an incipient cold: sneezes, a nose beginning to run with mucus, and a general chilly feeling making me want to put on more warm clothes than normally.

I get such colds about twice a year and they are no big deal. They are usually over within 48 hours, leaving only a cough that lasts another seven days. But the first 24 hours are the worst: I then usually put myself to bed with a hot-water bottle, a good book, the radio and an ample supply of hot drinks and paper handkerchiefs.

The trouble on this occasion was that I was catching within two hours the *Night Ferry* sleeping-car train to Paris, where I was due to lecture at a computer congress just when my cold would be at its worst. 'Would you like Mother to give you a healing?' asked my wife. 'Yes, please!' I replied, being as incompetent at self-healing as most conventional medical doctors. I then took myself off to Victoria Station and climbed into my sleeping-car bed well wrapped up in pyjamas and underwear.

One hour out of Victoria, when we were still only halfway to Dover, my nose suddenly cleared and I felt much too hot and overdressed. My mother-in-law had stopped my cold in its tracks, and I was able to give my lecture with a clear head and normal voice.

The Ideal Job

Five years ago, one of our coven members asked us to do some work for her uncle, an accountant who had been unemployed for over twelve months. He had written innumerable application letters, all without success, and was becoming depressed: he was beginning to drink more heavily, which would not improve his chances of finding work. His niece acting as the energy transmitter, we poured all our energy into him telepathically, sending him at the same time an image of proud self-confidence.

At our next meeting, we asked our member how her uncle was getting on. 'He got a job two weeks ago, and not just any job: *the* job he had always wanted at one of the best firms in his area.'

Saving the club

In 1945 Gerald Gardner had bought a few acres of Hertfordshire woodland on which to develop a nudist club, which was to be the cover for the witchcraft coven he would form with the initiates that wrote to him. But he had no interest in running the club itself, and appointed a salaried administrator to run the club on his behalf. This man deliberately ran the club at a loss by setting unrealistically high requirements for membership, hoping thereby to persuade Gerald eventually to sell the

164

club to him at a low price. But Gerald saw through the ploy, sacked the administrator and appointed his right-hand man in the coven, Jack Bracelin, in his place. This time he did not pay a salary, but told Jack he could live off the club's income.

The sacked administrator had not finished with us, however. He was a friend of Ernest Stanley, the puritanical owner of the North Kent naturist club and leading light in the Central Council of British Naturism (CCBN). He persuaded Stanley that under Jack's management our club was becoming a hotbed of witchcraft and loose living, and should be refused admission to the CCBN as well as advertising space in *Health and Efficiency*, the leading naturist monthly magazine. With all advertising refused to him, Jack got only a few new members in his first year of management and found it impossible to live off his management income. In January 1958, he asked us to work a spell to ensure a lifting of the advertising embargo.

Events now took a strange turn. A year earlier the Danish naturist magazine *Sun & Health* had run a forum on sexual education for naturists' children. I contributed an article recommending linking sex with love in the minds of children, but saying we should be consistent. When teenagers fell in love, they should be allowed to give their love a sexual expression, subject of course to the usual contraceptive precautions. Although I had written it as far back as July 1957, *Sun & Health* published it in their January 1958 issue.

This touched all of Ernest Stanley's most sensitive inhibitions. In the February 1958 issue of *Health & Efficiency* he published a libellous article accusing me of encouraging adult sexual abuse of children, and naming our club as front for 'witchcraft and black magic.' Jack's lawyer friend promptly slapped an injunction on all magazine distributors to stop distributing the magazine on pain of a libel suit. A day later, the offending issue disappeared from all newsagents' shelves.

Three weeks later, Jack received a letter from a firm of publishers informing him they had bought *Health & Efficiency* from the previous owners and had put a new editorial team in charge. They offered him three months' free advertising for his club, and normal commercial terms thereafter, if he would please lift the injunction on the magazine's distributors. The club was saved.

Healing Françoise (a case history already published in Tanya Luhrmann's *Persuasions of the Witch's Craft*)

In October 1958 I spent a week's vacation at the Brussels World Exhibition. On the last day, I sat opposite a pretty Belgian girl at lunch and we spent the afternoon touring the exhibition together. She informed me that she was epileptic and had an especially severe attack four years earlier, when she was 18. This had deprived her of her intellectual memory and she was unable to take any abstract or technical information in, but she didn't care: she was frozen in a state of superficial contentment. I commiserated and we parted after exchanging addresses.

It was only on the train back to London that it occurred to me that as an initiated witch I should be able to help Françoise with my coven's aid. So I wrote to her guardedly saying that my friends and I conducted experiments in spiritual healing. We were not very good at it, so could promise her nothing, except that at the worst it would make her no worse. If she was willing to co-operate, we would do what we could do for her. She should just send us a photograph and a lock of hair, pray to the Virgin Mary, and send us reports on her progress.

Our first working for Françoise took place on Saturday 1 November, when the full moon coincided with Halloween. Françoise's next letter reported that her intellectual memory was returning and her emotions had unfrozen: she was very depressed and spent hours weeping uncontrollably. She had frequent minor epileptic fits in which she fell down and promptly picked herself up again.

So we tried again at the next Full Moon meeting on 29 November. A week later our High Priestess Dayonis, Jack Bracelin and I were visiting two of our members at their home in Winchester when we decided to do an impromptu Wiccan

166

meeting. Whom to work for? Why, Françoise of course, with me once again as the energy transmitter. This time I heard irritated voices in my head saying: 'Stop bugging us! Your request for Françoise has been received and understood: now leave the rest to us. You can do no more.' When I got up, I told them what had happened and that we would not be working for Françoise any more.

In her next letter, Françoise reported an astonishing influx of energy. She had signed up for two university courses and was going out dancing every night. Then nothing for nearly six months.

In the spring of 1959 I had to make a business journey to Belgium. So I wrote to Françoise on the off-chance asking how she was, and whether I might visit her on the way. An enthusiastic reply came by return of post inviting me for the weekend and saying she and her mother would meet me off the boat at Ostend.

As I approached the car, her mother said she was so happy to meet the man who had healed Françoise.

'Healed? When?'

'Why, after my accident,' replied Françoise.

'What accident?'

'Oh! I suppose you don't know since I haven't written to you. On 24 January, I was being driven home from a ball by an escort who had had too much to drink. We had a head-on crash in which I was flung through the windscreen. I was in coma for five days and needed 13 stitches to my scalp (she showed me the scars of some), but when I came to, I was cured of epilepsy. I haven't had a fit since then.'

On returning to London I checked with a medical doctor in our coven, who confirmed that epilepsy is a faulty circuit in the brain, which can often be cured by a sudden traumatic shock. Unfortunately, the effects are wholly random (my friend could easily have been killed or crippled by her accident) so that it is not possible to base a therapy on this knowledge. Unfortunately, I then lost touch with Françoise so I don't know whether the cure held. She was beginning to fall in love with me, and I had to either marry her or break off the relationship.

167

There is something for everybody in this story. A psychologist would say that the original emotional unfreezing was due to the encouragement that an eligible young man was taking an interest in her. As for the car accident, it was bound to happen sooner or later to someone who went dancing every night at a time when Belgians did not require driving licences. A Roman Catholic would say it was a miracle in answer to Françoise's prayers to the Virgin Mary.

But the unseen powers who fulfil Wiccan magical wishes had left their signature on the cure. Françoise's accident happened two nights before the next Full Moon, and she needed thirteen stitches in her head (13 is the number of lunar months in a solar year and thus a sacred number for witches).

Her Deepest Wish Fulfilled

Most of our coven celebrated Yule 1961 with the family of two of our members in Folkestone. One of the participants was Jane, a merry and passionate but unhappily married woman whose husband had become psychologically impotent after being present at the birth of her second son. She consoled herself by having plenty of extra-marital affairs. On this occasion, she confided that she had fallen in love with a young married policeman in her home town. 'I don't want to break up his marriage, but could you cast a spell so that he notices me and comes to see me discreetly occasionally.'

People are forever asking us to cast this sort of love spell but it is strictly against Wiccan ethics. Quite apart from the danger to the young man's marriage (wives always find out) and his career (British police forces don't tolerate adultery among their officers), we regard it as akin to psychic rape to cast a spell on anybody without their consent, except in emergency circumstances like for the victim of an accident in coma. So we refused to work on the police officer. But so as not to make Jane feel let down and abandoned, we worked for her instead and asked the Goddess to grant her 'her deepest wish.'

Five weeks later Jane met Bill and they fell in love. She divorced her impotent husband, married Bill, gave up her extra-marital flings, and they are still happily married today, thirty-five years later.

The Brazilian Shaman

In October 1968 my family were invited to the Hampstead home of Gerda Boyesen, a Reichian psychotherapist, to attend a healing session given by the visiting Brazilian medium, Lorival de Freitas. We took our two children along, including our then five-year old deaf daughter Helen, in the hope he might do something for her. While her hearing loss is almost total she has a great gift for lip-reading, but she was restless at the time and my wife found it very hard to get her to concentrate.

A quiet tall mestizo by nature, Lorival needed to down half a bottle of neat whisky to get going. He then became possessed by the spirit of the emperor Nero, who was atoning for his crimes on Earth by healing people from the other side via mediums. 'Nero' needed the energy of a fiesta to conduct his healings, so the thirty-odd guests at the party spent their time dancing to rock music when they were not being healed.

The first healings were spectacular. Our host's daughter, Mona Lisa, a ballet dancer, had been unable to dance because of crippling pains in her back. 'Nero' told her to strip to her waist, and then slashed her back in an X shape with a cut-throat razor. He then applied an empty glass to her back, squeezed her back, and showed the audience the glass filled with what looked like wet cotton wool. 'This is the ectoplasm I have just extracted from Mona Lisa's back. Now she will be able to dance!' He passed his hand over her back, and the slash wounds immediately disappeared. Mona Lisa shook herself, dressed again and spent the rest of the evening dancing wildly.

An elderly man suffering from a cataract now came forward. 'Nero' operated on his eyes with a pocket penknife, and the man could see again normally. Other healings followed but I cannot remember the details.

169

At last Helen's turn came. 'Nero' sat her on his knee and explained through an interpreter that her physical deafness was karmic against which he was powerless; but he would help her communicate despite her deafness. 'I am now going to put her to sleep, and in a few minutes one of the guests – I don't know who – will sing to her soul.' He now took out a pendulum and swung it in front of Helen's eyes. Within a minute she was asleep and he laid her on the floor.

Suddenly from the back of the watching group a Belgian visitor began singing an operatic aria in a magnificent baritone voice. Within a minute, Helen started beating the rhythm with her feet in her sleep and her face broke in a blissful smile. When the aria ended she woke up and ran into 'Nero's' arms and kissed him passionately. Thereafter my wife had no more problems getting Helen to concentrate in her lip-reading and speaking lessons. Within two years, her speech was almost normal and her vocabulary had caught up with her hearing contemporaries.

Weather Magic

I first came across successful weather magic at the Pagan Spirit Gathering in Wisconsin in June 1988. The whole Middle West was suffering from an oppressive heat wave and drought punctuated by occasional thunderstorms. One had closed Chicago O'Hare airport for three hours on the day of my arrival and my plane had to be diverted to Milwaukee.

At the opening assembly and ritual on a clear cloudless evening we were warned that our campsite was a tinderbox and a spark could set it alight. Fires – a favourite Pagan ritual stage setting – were absolutely forbidden, except in metal containers well off the ground and with a gallon of water close by. At the end of the ritual we conducted a weather magic ritual asking the gods to divert our way one of the thunderstorms predicted for North Wisconsin 100 miles from our camp site. Then we all repaired to our tents.

I was woken at 3 a.m. by claps of thunder and a torrential downpour of rain, which my tent fortunately withstood. This went on until 5 a.m. and resumed from 6 o'clock to 7.30 a.m., leaving the campsite sodden. But by 8 o'clock the sun was shining again and by 10 a.m. the ground was again dry. Later the shopping party who bought food for the whole camp in the nearby town reported there had been no trace of rain within five miles of our campsite: the storm had been entirely local.

Taking off for Peru

In October 1990, I joined a group of sixteen Californian Pagans on a ten-day trip to the Peruvian temples of the Inca period. We flew from San Francisco to Los Angeles, where we connected with an Argentinian flight to Lima. Five minutes after we landed, fog closed LA International airport to all landings and take-offs. There was an enormous queue in front of the Aerolineas Argentinas check-in desk, as the airline was checking nobody in until their aircraft had landed.

Leaving one member of the party to look after our luggage, the rest of us went outside the terminal to a grass knoll and conducted a ritual to blow the fog away to sea. Within five minutes a light breeze began to blow towards the sea, and after a further five minutes gaps began to appear in the cloud sitting on the airport. We then ended the ritual and returned to the terminal, to find the queue almost gone: they had started checking people in five minutes before.

We still had to wait two hours before the aircraft was ready to take off again. During this time I went to the arrivals hall to reserve a rented car for my return to LA ten days later. On the arrivals panel, every incoming flight from Latin America except ours was marked as cancelled or diverted.

Commanding the English weather

Nine months later, in June 1991, I attended a gathering of some 120 European Wiccans in the English Lake District, one of the most beautiful but also rainiest parts of the country. On the first evening we trudged ten minutes across fields from our guest house to the meadow where the opening ritual was planned. Apart from the odd cirrus cloud the sky was clear. I was in the outer circle with no ritual role to play.

As the ritual proceeded, my eyes wandered to a tall hill in the south, where I suddenly saw a black thundercloud emerge from over the hill heading in our direction. If this goes on, I thought, this cloud will be over us in five minutes, open up and we will be drenched before we can get back to the guest house. So focusing my eyes intently on the cloud I said silently: 'Stop! Stay where you are! Respect the boundaries of the circle!' The cloud stopped and stayed in the same spot for five minutes. So I relaxed my concentration and returned to pay attention to the ritual.

After another five minutes, I checked on my cloud to find that wisps of it were beginning to reach in our direction, like a dog who puts first one paw and then another on a bed that he knows he shouldn't climb on. Once more I concentrated on the cloud and held it in its position for the next twenty minutes. It then dispersed to the east and the west, and by the end of the ritual the whole surrounding sky had turned grey, except for that part immediately above our ritual site.

For the next four days we enjoyed dry sunny weather, but on the last day we awoke to find it raining. A Midsummer ritual at a nearby stone circle had been planned for the morning, but was postponed until the afternoon in case the rain stopped. A dozen of us then got together and conducted a weather ritual in the rain, asking the rain to hold off long enough for us to conduct our ritual in the afternoon.

At 1.30 p.m. the rain stopped, and the organisers decided we would hold our planned ritual at the stone circle at 3 p.m. We walked there in dry weather; started on time at 3 o'clock. The ritual lasted 90 minutes and at half past four we closed the circle and returned to our clothes. Five minutes later, it started raining again and went on raining all evening.

Powerless Against Nerthus's displeasure

Like all forms of magic and indeed all human endeavour, weather magic doesn't always work: we need to have the Goddess or the local raingod on our side. A year later, at the next European Wiccan gathering in Western Norway, we had rainy weather for most of the week as I have already mentioned in a previous chapter. I again tried weather magic with some fellow Wiccans, but the rain clouds racing in from the North Sea took no notice. Nerthus, the goddess of the land, wanted to teach us not to ignore Her, and against Her displeasure we were powerless.

High Magic

Many of the Western Mysteries magical lodges despise the spells we practise and call it 'low magic'. They concentrate instead on 'high magic' which is mostly concerned with making contact with their own higher selves, or – in the sonorous words of Aleister Crowley – 'attaining the knowledge and conversation of the Holy Guardian Angel.' Why such self-centred magic should be regarded as 'higher' and worthier than healing and helping others, or even influencing the weather for the benefit of one's friends, has always puzzled me.

When ceremonial magical lodges engage in instrumental magic, it is usually of a very ambitious kind, such as 'injecting ideas of Justice into the nation's collective unconscious'. Worthy though such an aim is, how on earth do they get their feedback and know they have succeeded? There is also quite a disparity between the collective energy of a dozen magicians in a lodge and the collective unconscious of 50 million people, or even the few thousand members of its ruling class. On one occasion, however, a piece of high magic achieved spectacular results.

The Harmonic Convergence

In 1986, the American writer Jose Arguelles wrote that according to the Mayan calendar a *harmonic convergence* of astrological and earth energies would take place on 15 August 1987 which would give humanity a choice between two different futures: either war and the destruction of civilisation, or a peaceful transition to a new age. The world was still frozen in the Cold War at the time and thermonuclear arsenals with the power to kill all life on Earth five times over were still being added to, so the possibility of a uniquely destructive world war was not too fanciful.

The coming Harmonic Convergence was widely publicised in all New Age and esoteric circles, and even got coverage in daily papers. The cartoonist Doonesbury took it up and called it the 'Moronic Conversion'. So on 15 August 1987, Pagans, New Agers, esotericists and Peace activists of all religions around the world climbed up their nearest hill or mountain and at the given hour all prayed, meditated or worked magic for the sake of Peace.

Nothing happened immediately (to Boopsie's disappointment in the Doonesbury cartoon). But only four months later, in November 1987, the Soviet government announced it would withdraw its troops from Afghanistan. The following year, the Soviets started disarming unilaterally, forcing the West to follow suit. In 1989, two years after the Harmonic Convergence, Communism collapsed in Eastern Europe making way for democracy.

In August 1991, four years exactly after the Harmonic Convergence, the Moscow coup against President Gorbachev failed and Communist rule in Russia came to an end, followed shortly after by the Soviet Union's break-up. Today, a further five years on, the world is an immeasurably safer place than at the time of the Harmonic Convergence, despite all the horrors taking place in Bosnia, Somalia, Rwanda and Burundi.

Obviously I don't claim that the collaborative high magic that took place on 15 August 1987 was alone responsible for ending the Cold War. People at the highest echelons of the

American and Soviet governments worked to this end for over a decade. President Gorbachev had made concrete proposals to President Reagan at their first meeting in Iceland. But always until then, the forces of peace had been overruled on both sides by the forces of mutual distrust or the interests of the two military-industrial complexes. What those working for peace at the Harmonic Convergence may have achieved was to give just that extra spiritual boost to the forces of peace to enable them to win the day.

Magical Ethics

I have already mentioned that it is strictly against Wiccan ethics to cast a spell on any person without their consent, except in a life-threatening emergency. Some New Agers are against any form of instrumental magic, even for good. To heal a person might be to deprive her or him of the lessons her/his illness was intended to teach her/him. To influence the weather magically could have unforeseen and undesirable ecological consequences.

You could use the same argument against any form of human activity, including medicine, agriculture and gardening. Why should it be more wrong to heal a person with the power of the mind than with antibiotics? Agriculture, roads and industry have more far-reaching and lasting ecological effects than a temporary weather spell.

Generally, if it is right to do something using mundane means, like healing, then it is equally right to do it magically if one knows how, and magic like homoeopathy has none of allopathic drugs' side-effects. If it is wrong to coerce another person with physical force, then it is equally wrong to coerce them with the power of the mind.

If Wiccans have fewer inhibitions against spellcasting than some sections of the New Age, it is also because we know that we are not magically omnipotent. Our spells work if we invoke the power of the Goddess or one of the local gods to aid us, and they won't if our spell would go against a higher good.

175

The Importance of Spells

The gods also have their reasons for letting us rediscover the power of spellcasting with which our tribal ancestors were familiar. Contemporary science and technology are experimenting with ever more dangerous techniques: more potent chemicals, nuclear energy and genetic engineering to name but a few. Whatever safety measures scientists claim to be taking, Chernobyl has proved the truth of Murphy's Law: 'Whatever can go wrong, will go wrong.'

When the next Chernobyl happens, an ability to deflect radioactive clouds from where one is living could come in handy. When a deadly virus escapes from a laboratory and spreads epidemically around the world, spiritual healing and self-healing with the Goddess' help may be the only thing that might help us to escape. Competence in healing and spellcasting may well be our entrance ticket to the next Noah's Ark.

13

The Sacred Marriage

The Third (High Priest(ess)) Degree

In Wicca, as in medieval craft guilds, attaining the third and highest degree of elevation entitles a Wiccan to 'hive off' from her coven and form her own. In what is known of 19th century and earlier covens (very little), the title of the head of a coven was Mistress, Master or Magister, unless (s)he belonged to the aristocracy, in which case (s)he would be called the Lady or Lord of the coven.

Twentieth-century Wicca has taken from ceremonial magic the titles High Priestess and High Priest. Wicca is unique among magical orders in that the head of a coven is normally a High Priestess, though here too there can be exceptions. It is she who formally hives off from her parent coven to form her own, and will normally take with her those coven members who feel closest to her. She can then appoint any Second or Third degree man to be her High Priest partner for one meeting or on a more permanent basis.

In practice, however, the most stable covens are those with a committed couple at their head, and they will normally meet at the High Priestess's and High Priest's home when they are not meeting out of doors in some wood or sacred site. In the covens to which I have belonged, the High Priestess's home is not just the meeting place for formal indoor Full Moon meetings. It is also a social centre, where apprentices drop in to copy their *Book of Shadows* and make their magical tools under the High Priest(ess)'s guidance, plan an open seasonal festival, or just chat about magical topics or current affairs.

The pre-eminence of the High Priestess has given most Wiccan covens their close family atmosphere, in which there is a delicate balance between an informal consensus among all the coven's members, which is then articulated firmly by the High Priestess. The male-led magical lodges that I know tend to veer to either of two extremes. The lodge is led either by an *adept*, who is alone in communication with the *inner plane adepti* or Hidden Masters and whose orders are obeyed without question by the lodge's other members. Or it is a hotbed of intrigue and jockeying for position among the more experienced men, each trying to come out on top.

The Sacred Marriage

Covens differ in their requirements for the Third degree of Wicca, though all would include interpersonal skills and a proven ability to lead a coven. But the formal *masterpiece* that a companion witch has to achieve before being elevated to the status of High Priest(ess) is the ultimate ego-transcendence of being able to channel the Goddess or the Horned God during a meeting.

When both the High Priestess and the High Priest channel the two deities simultaneously, they should be able to perform the Sacred Marriage, Wicca's highest sacrament: a ritual sexual union between the Goddess and the Horned God that will ensure the land's fertility and the whole coven's close communion with the two deities. If Tantric sexual meditation techniques are employed, the union's climax itself can catapult the two partners into a state of cosmic consciousness, as I discovered in the arms of my first companion 40 years ago.

Many gay men and lesbians have complained that the central role played by this heterosexual union between High Priestess and High Priest makes them feel left out, and that Wicca is therefore 'homophobic'. Some individuals may be, but I can assure them that the movement as such is not. I know a number of gay men, lesbians and bisexuals in Wicca who have achieved a high degree of spirituality and are magically very effective.

What the Sacred Marriage as the supreme Wiccan sacrament affirms is the sacredness of sexual desire and sexual union, after centuries of Christian repression in which they were the great unmentionables. To heterosexuals – who are after all a majority in both Wicca and the population at large – such a union of the complementary opposites, Goddess and God, can only be meaningfully enacted by a woman and a man: after all, only heterosexual unions can perpetuate life on Earth. It is up to gay men and lesbians to create sacraments and rituals that would be equally meaningful to them and to the other members of any mixed covens to which they may belong.

In most covens only committed partners perform the Sacred Marriage. A symbolic union takes place at the elevation ritual between the High Priest(ess) and the member being raised to the Third Degree, unless of course they are in a committed partnership.

A few covens, however, feel that the strong emotional bonds created by sexual intimacy should not be limited to monogamous partnerships, but can weld the core of a coven into a highly effective magical team. The real Sacred Marriage at Third Degree elevation will be the entry into this inner core. Their close emotional bonds tend to give such covens great stability, sometimes extending over decades, but are not very conducive to hiving off, so that they tend to spawn few daughter covens.

This may have been standard practice in the witch covens of earlier times, which would explain why the stag horns that Wiccan high priests wear when the Horned God is called down on them have become in France the symbol of the cuckolded husband.

The Sacred Prostitute

In America some Goddess worshipping women – not all of them Wiccan – have felt impelled to take the sacredness of sex a stage further, and explore the role of the *sacred prostitute*: the priestess in the temple of Ishtar in Babylon or of Aphrodite in Corinth, who was available to any man who wished to experience the sacred marriage within the temple.

In contemporary society, that would not be the streetwalker nor even the high-class call girl, but the sexual therapist who heals diffident and psychically impotent men who have been unable to form personal relationships. That is a vital role in contemporary mass society in which there is so much loneliness and misery, and in which the blind aggression and pursuit of power that sexual frustration so often produces, is potentially so lethal to the survival of the human race.

It is, however, a vocation for only a small number of sexually self-confident women with plenty of spiritual stamina: it is certainly no part of the responsibilities of the average Wiccan High Priestess.

A Healing

Let me conclude as I began this book with a personal experience. My first wife died in July 1986 and I was still grieving for her when I flew to America to attend the annual Pagan Spirit Gathering in Wisconsin in June 1987. There I met again Susan, whom I had met six years earlier. She was alone, her regular partner having business commitments.

I was staying in a nearby motel, which meant I had to leave the campsite no later than midnight. But on the third night, a wild and exuberant dance that followed a fire ritual was still in full swing when the midnight hour approached. Susan invited me to sleep in her tent if I did not want to leave the dance then.

As we bedded down, she suddenly looked at me and asked:

'Do you still grieve for Gillian?'

'Yes!'

'Does it hurt?'

180

'Yes, when I think of her,' and my eyes filled with tears.

'Then let me give you the Goddess' healing!'

Gently and tenderly she took me in her arms and made love to me all night. When we woke in the morning it was raining and there didn't seem much point in getting up, so we made love some more.

With that act of love, Susan healed my soul and reconnected me with the life-stream as nothing else could have done. I shall always remember it with deep gratitude.

Conclusion

This healing was within the ethical outlook of the Earth Goddess religion, and probably of few other contemporary faiths. It expressed the primacy that Goddess worshippers put on the values of the heart, and our lack of shame to express these physically where appropriate. Cerridwen Fallingstar mentions a similar episode in her past life recall novel, *The Heart of the Fire*.

But again I am not proposing this as a general Wiccan High Priestess duty to all bereaved men in their covens. Every coven and individual within it is unique, and has the Goddess-given freedom to respond to each unique situation in its own way. How many other religions and esoteric movements can say the same?

Bibliography

I The End of Absolutes

Birnbaum, Norman and Gertrud Lenzer. *Sociology and Religion*, Prentice-Hall

Bocock, Robert and Kenneth Thompson. *Religion and Ideology*, 1985

Fox, Matthew. *Original Blessing. A Primer in Creation Spirituality*, 1983
  The Coming of the Cosmic Christ, Harper & Row, 1988

Freud, Sigmund. *Moses and Monotheism*, Amsterdam, 1939; London, 1964

James, William. *The Varieties of Religious Experience*, London, 1902

Macfarlane, Alan. *The Origins of English Individualism*, 1978

Maslow, Abraham H. *Religions, Values and Peak Experiences*, Penguin, 1987

Tawney, R. H. *Religion and the Rise of Capitalism*, London, 1926

Weber, Max. *The Protestant Ethic and the Spirit of Capitalism*, London, 1930
  The Sociology of Religion, Boston, 1963

II The Worship of Life

Adler, Margot. *Drawing Down the Moon. Witches, Druids, Goddess-Worshippers and Other Pagans in America Today*, 1979, 1986

Apuleius, Lucius. *The Golden Ass*, translated by Robert Graves, 1951

Ashe, Geoffrey. *The Virgin*, Paladin, 1977

Aswynn, Freya. *Leaves of Yggdrasil*, London, 1988

Bailey, Alice A. *A Treatise on White Magic*, Lucis Press, 1974

Barrett, Clive. *The Viking Gods*, Aquarian, London, 1989

Bhagwan Shree Rajneesh. *The Book of the Secrets*
The Supreme Doctrine
The Way of the White Cloud and other writings, Rajneesh Foundation

Bloom, William. (ed.) *The New Age, An Anthology of Essential Writings*, 1991

Crowley, Vivianne. *Phoenix from the Flame*, Aquarian/Thorson, 1994
Principles of Paganism, Thorsons, 1996

De Grandis, Francesca. *Goddess Wisdom, a Celtic Shaman's Guide*, HarperCollins, 1997

Eisler, Riane. *The Chalice and the Blade*, Harper & Row, San Francisco, 1987

Farrar, Janet and Stewart. *The Witches' Goddess*, Robert Hale, London, 1987
The Witches' God, Robert Hale, London, 1989
Eight Sabbats for Witches

Ferguson, Marilyn. *The Aquarian Conspiracy*, Paladin, London, 1982

Gardner, Gerald B. *Witchcraft Today*, London, 1954

Gimbutas, Marija. *The Language of the Goddess*, Harper & Row, 1989
The Goddess and Gods of Old Europe, Berkeley, 1974

Gonzales-Wippler, Migene. *Santeria. African Magic in Latin America*, 1981
Santeria, the Religion, Llewellyn, St Paul, 1994

Graichen, Gisella. *Die Neuen Hexen*, Hoffmann und Campe, Hamburg, 1986

Hardman, Charlotte and Graham Harvey, (eds) *Paganism Today*, Thorsons, 1996

Hutton, Ronald. *The Pagan Religions of the Ancient British Isles*, 1991

Jones, Prudence and Caitlin Matthews, (eds.) *Voices from the Circle*, 1990

Jones, Prudence and Nigel Pennick. *A History of Pagan Europe*, 1995

Keen, Sam. *To a Dancing God*, Harper & Row, San Francisco, 1970

Matthews, Caitlin. *The Elements of the Celtic Tradition*, Element, 1989

Matthews, Caitlin. (ed.) *Voices of the Goddess*, Aquarian, London, 1990

Ochs, Carol. *Behind the Sex of God*, Beacon Press, Boston, 1977

O'Regan, Vivienne. *The Pillar of Isis*, Aquarian/Thorson, London, 1992

Ozaniec, Naomi. *Daughter of the Goddess*, Aquarian/Thorson, London, 1993

Robert. *The Divine Struggle*, Nemeton, Berkeley CA, 1990

Robertson, Olivia. *The Call of Isis*, Cesara Publications, Ireland, 1975

Ruppert, Hans-Jürgen. *Die Hexen kommen. Magie und Hexenglaube heute.*, Wiesbaden, 1987

Sjöö, Monica and Barbara Mor. *The Great Cosmic Mother*, Bristol, 1975

Starhawk. *The Spiral Dance. A Rebirth of the Ancient Religion of the Great Goddess*, Harper & Row, San Francisco, 1979, 1987

Stewart, R. J. *Celtic Gods, Celtic Goddesses*, Blandford, London, 1990

Stone, Merlin. *The Paradise Papers*, Virago Press, London, 1976

Trevelyan, Sir George. *A Vision of the Aquarian Age*, Coventure, 1977

Watts, Alan. *The Way of Zen*, New York, 1957
The Supreme Identity, Faber & Faber, London, 1972

Whitmont, Edward C. *Return of the Goddess*, Routledge, London, 1983

III Handling Power

Arguelles, Jose. *The Mayan Factor*, 1986

Bonewits, P. E. I. *Real Magic*, Berkeley, 1970

Camus, Dominique. *Pouvoirs sorciers*, Imago, Paris, 1988

Crowley, Vivianne. *Wicca, the Old Religion in the New Age*, Aquarian, 1989

Fallingstar, Cerridwen. *The Heart of the Fire, a novel*, California, 1990

Gardner, Gerald B. *The Meaning of Witchcraft*, London, 1959

Green, Marian. *A Witch Alone*, Aquarian, London, 1991

Hurcombe, Linda. (ed.) *Sex and God: Some Varieties of Women's Religious Experience*, Routledge, London, 1987

Jones, Evan John and Doreen Valiente, *Witchcraft, a Tradition Renewed*, 1990

Leland, Charles G. *Aradia, Gospel of the Witches*, 1899, reprinted 1974

Lethbridge, T. C. *Witches. Investigating an Ancient Religion*, Routledge, 1962

Luhrmann, Tanya M. *Persuasions of the Witch's Craft*, Blackwell, 1989

May, Rollo. *Love and Will*, Collins, London, 1972

Michelet, Jules. *La Sorcière*, Paris, 1861 reprinted 1987

Montaigu, *Panorama de l'art du sorcier*, Paris, 1979

Murray, Margaret. *The Witch Cult in Western Europe*, 1924
The God of the Witches, 1933

Qualls-Corbett, Nancy. *The Sacred Prostitute: Eternal Aspects of the Feminine*, Toronto, 1988

Valiente, Doreen. *The Rebirth of Witchcraft*, Robert Hale, London, 1989